Simple Dinners

Simple Dinners

MURDOCH
BOOKS

42

93

155

contents

special features

Using this book

Simple Dinners is a collection of evening meals that are easy to prepare, use a limited number of ingredients (readily available from most large supermarkets) and, most importantly, are extremely tasty.

Kitchen staples

Canned fish—anchovies, tuna, salmon
Canned peeled Roma tomatoes—whole and chopped
Canned pulses—lentils, chickpeas, butter beans
Capers
Chillies—dried and fresh
Chocolate—dark and milk
Cocoa powder
Coconut milk and cream
Dry breadcrumbs
Frozen pastry shells, pastry sheets, pizza bases
Frozen vegetables—peas, chopped onions, corn
Fruit—canned and dried
Garlic—fresh
Ginger—fresh
Herbs—dried oregano, bay leaves, mixed Italian
Lemon—fresh or frozen cubes of juice
Meats—salami, chorizo, bacon
Mustards—Dijon, wholegrain
Noodles—dried, long-life
Nuts—pine nuts, almonds, walnuts
Oils—extra virgin olive, olive, vegetable
Olives
Pasta—dried or frozen filled pasta (e.g. ravioli)
Pastes—sambal oelek or another chilli paste, curry pastes (red and green), laksa pastes
Rice—long-grain, arborio, jasmine
Sauces—soy, fish, oyster, hoisin, sweet chilli, Tabasco, Worcestershire
Spices—cumin, coriander, paprika, cayenne, cinnamon, nutmeg, peppercorns, curry powder
Stock—chicken, vegetable, beef, fish
Tomato paste
Vinegar—balsamic, red wine, white wine
Wine—white and red

A guide to the recipes

We have divided our recipes into chapters to help you easily work out what you want to cook. For the most part, the chapters are grouped together by the main ingredient—chicken, beef and veal, lamb, pork, seafood, pasta and rice—so that you can flick through a chapter for ideas using a certain ingredient. In addition, there is a chapter on vegetarian food, one full of great accompaniments, such as salads and a chapter featuring delicious desserts.

Most of the recipes need very little cooking and will be on the table in no time. But don't be alarmed when you see that some meals (for example, casseroles, stews and some roasts) require longer to cook. These recipes are included in this book of simple dinners because they take almost no time to prepare and, once they are on to cook, they look after themselves.

You will notice that some recipes specify a time for marinating; this time is a guide for maximum flavour, but it can be shortened if you are short of time.

A well-stocked kitchen

For fuss-free cooking, start with a well-stocked kitchen. Apart from a few fresh items that need to be bought on a regular basis, a well-stocked freezer, fridge and pantry means you should never be stuck for something simple to make for dinner. See the adjacent list for a comprehensive list of foods to keep on hand.

Shopping hints for quick cooking

- You can save a lot of time by buying pre-cut meat. Most butchers and supermarkets have marinated sliced meat for stir-frying and cubed meats for casseroles (take care because some pre-cut meats can be quite fatty).
- Frozen vegetables are very handy and can save a lot of time. Another option is one of the many pre-prepared stir-fry packs of vegetables now sold by most large supermarkets.
- A large range of stir-fry sauces is available from the supermarket, so once you have mastered the stir-fries in this book, vary them with different sauces.

- Packets of pre-grated cheese can save a lot of preparation time.
- Frozen pre-rolled pastry sheets make an ideal base for a quick fruit tart or savoury pizza.
- Buying frozen cooked rice is an even quicker option than cooking your own. Follow the manufacturer's instructions to reheat.
- Ready-cooked barbecue chickens from your local barbecue chicken shop or supermarket are ideal for making quick pizzas, pasta dishes or warm salads. Simply remove the meat and skin from the bones and shred with your fingers.
- Pre-cooked pastry shells available from supermarkets make easy desserts—fill with ice cream or canned fruits.
- Stocks are a common liquid base to many dishes, and for optimum flavour, it is often recommended to make your own. However, good-quality liquid stocks are available in tetra packs or in cans. Canned stocks are available from Asian stores or the Asian section of most large supermarkets. They can be a little salty, so use half water, half stock, if desired.
- Bottled pasta sauces are readily available and make life wonderfully simple. Add your personal touch by adding fresh herbs, olives or flaked canned tuna.

Basic cooking tips

- Plan ahead: read through your recipe and assemble all the equipment and ingredients that you need before you start.
- Decide on any side dishes or accompaniments you wish to serve, and where possible, prepare them while cooking the main meal. Many dishes, such as stir-fries, curries and pan-fries, are accompanied by rice, which takes about 15 minutes to cook. To maximise time usage, start cooking the rice before you start preparing the rest of your meal.
- When you are making a casserole or stew, you can make double quantities and freeze half in meal-sized portions. Remove a portion from the freezer in the morning and thaw in the fridge.
- If cooking with a wok, make sure that it is hot before the oil and food are added. This ensures that the cooking time is short, and the ingredients—especially the meat—will be seared instantly, sealing in the juices.
- Stir-frying is one of the fastest cooking methods, but it's important to have all your ingredients measured and prepared before you start cooking because the wok should not be left unattended.

Kitchen basics

Part of the secret to a well-stocked kitchen is knowing how to store and cook your produce to ensure it stays in good condition for as long as possible.

meat

■ Meat will keep for 2–3 days in the fridge. Remove it from its packaging as soon as you get it home, transfer to a clean plate, cover with plastic wrap and store in the coldest part of the fridge. Large roasting joints should be placed on a rack over a plate.

■ Use minced meat within 24 hours of purchase.

■ To freeze meat, place it in freezer bags and expel all the air. Never re-freeze thawed meat.

■ Thaw meat in the fridge or by carefully following your microwave's instruction manual. Chops and steaks will thaw in about 5 hours, while larger joints will need to be thawed at least overnight.

■ Never cook partially frozen meat. Although the outer layers cook and become brown, the interior will remain cool and enable potentially dangerous bacteria to develop.

■ To make it easier to slice meat thinly for stir-fries, freeze the meat for 30 minutes. Do not do this with meat that has already been frozen and thawed, as it could lead to food poisoning.

■ If you like your steak rare to medium, buy steaks cut as thick as possible (about 5 cm/2 inch) to ensure that they do not overcook.

■ When cooking steaks, a quick test for doneness is to press the steak as it cooks with your index finger—if it feels soft and flexible it is rare, if it gives a little it is medium and if it is firm and does not spring back at all then it is well done.

■ For a larger joint, test for doneness by inserting a skewer into the thickest part of the meat, then remove it and press the surface hard with the skewer to check the colour of the juices that run out. If the juices are faintly red then the meat will be rare, if they are faintly pink, the meat will be cooked medium, and if the juices are clear then the meat will be well done.

Guide to roasting times at 180°C (350°F/Gas 4)	
Rare	20–25 minutes per 500 g (1 lb)
Medium	25–30 minutes per 500 g (1 lb)
Well done	30–35 minutes per 500 g (1 lb)

chicken

■ Chicken will keep for 2–3 days in the fridge. Always put the chicken on a clean plate or tray, cover with plastic wrap or foil and place on the bottom shelf of the fridge so that it does not drip on other food. Whole chickens should be placed on a rack over a plate to ensure that they are not sitting in a pool of their own juices.

■ When freezing chicken, wrap tightly in plastic wrap and expel any excess air. Never re-freeze chicken unless it has been cooked first.

■ Always thaw chicken in the fridge or by following your microwave's instruction manual. Chicken pieces will thaw in about 5 hours, while whole chickens will need to be thawed at least overnight.

■ Never cook chicken that is partially frozen.

■ To check if a whole chicken is cooked, insert a skewer into the flesh between the thigh and the breast—if the juices run clear then the bird is cooked.

■ Chicken pieces on or off the bone are fully cooked when they feel springy when touched with your finger.

seafood

■ All seafood should be eaten within 2 days, assuming that it was very fresh when bought. If you can't be sure of the freshness, then it is best to eat it on the same day.

■ Pat the fish dry and store it in an airtight bag or a plate in the coldest part of the refrigerator.

■ Keep mussels and clams in a bucket or on a tray covered with a damp cloth.

■ Keep prawns and scallops in a sealed container.

■ Only freeze fish that is very fresh. Freeze unpeeled prawns by covering them with water, to form a large ice block. Fish will freeze for up to 3 months—freezer burn deteriorates it after this. Never re-freeze seafood.

■ Most seafood is cooked when it turns opaque. Whole fish or fillets of fish are cooked when a knife inserted into the centre slips in with little or no resistance, or the flesh flakes easily with a knife.

- Some fish (for example, tuna and Atlantic salmon) is best served still rare in the centre to stop it drying out.
- Molluscs should be cooked only until the shells open—if cooked for longer, the meat will become tough and rubbery. For this reason, it is best to cook molluscs in small batches and remove them from the pan as soon as they open.
- Small octopus, cuttlefish and squid require very little cooking—cook them just until they turn opaque. To ensure that they remain tender, cook them over high heat for a brief time. Larger octopus, squid and cuttlefish require a long simmering process to tenderise them.

vegetables

- Most vegetables can be stored in the vegetable drawers of your refrigerator for up to 1 week. Root vegetables should be stored in a cool, dry and airy place and will keep for 2–3 weeks.
- Lettuce will remain crisp and firm in a lettuce crisper or sealed freezer bag.
- Wash vegetables just before using to avoid them rotting if stored when damp.
- Fresh herbs should be wrapped in damp kitchen paper then stored in an airtight bag in the fridge.
- Most fresh vegetables are not suited to freezing raw. If you want to take advantage of a seasonal glut of produce, trim or peel the vegetables (such as beans, broccoli, carrots or peas), lightly blanch them, then drain and seal in ziplock bags before freezing.

fruit

- Most fruit is best kept in the fridge once it ripens; although bananas and citrus prefer room temperature.
- Bananas that are past their best can be peeled and frozen in ziplock bags and used for smoothies or cakes.
- Store unripe avocados in a paper bag in a cool, dark place to encourage ripening.
- Buy fresh fruit every few days to gain the best possible flavour. Remember that buying fruit which is in season will not only mean it will taste much better, but it will also be cheaper than out of season fruit.
- If you have any leftover lemon juice, freeze it in ice cube trays in tablespoon portions.

dairy and eggs

- Wrap blocks of cheese in foil or kitchen paper and store in the dairy compartment of your fridge. Any exposure to air will dry out the cheese and spoil it.
- Grated cheese can be frozen for up to 3 months if stored in airtight bags.
- Eggs are best kept in the refrigerator and taken out 30 minutes before you want to use them. Store them in the cartons rather than in the egg compartment of your fridge—their porous shells mean that they easily absorb the flavours of strong-smelling foods. Eggs should be stored pointy-side-down to protect the air sac at the other end which keeps them fresh.

pantry items

- Store dry ingredients, such as flour, sugar and nuts in an airtight container, as kitchen pests, such as weevils and cockroaches, can be a problem in open packets.
- Check the labels of jars and condiments to ensure they don't need refrigeration after opening.
- Spices lose their flavour over time, so buy them in small quantities and check the use-by date regularly.
- To store pastes (such as tomato and curry) for longer periods of time in convenient small portions, spoon them into ice-cube trays, then freeze, divide into plastic bags and keep in the freezer until ready to use.
- Transform any stale pieces of bread into breadcrumbs by processing the slices in a food processor. Freeze in ziplock bags for up to 6 months.

cakes and desserts

- To test whether a cake or sponge-based pudding is cooked, insert a skewer into the centre and if it comes out clean then it is cooked.
- Cooking times will vary from oven to oven. As a general rule, fan-forced ovens cook more quickly and have a more even overall heat.
- If you don't have exactly the right-sized tin, it may not matter. A 1 cm (1/2 inch) difference will not ruin a pie or tart; you may just have a little too much or not enough filling, so adjust it accordingly.

chicken

14 steamed chicken breast with asian greens

ingredients

- 10 g (1/4 oz) dried Chinese mushrooms
- 2 tablespoons soy sauce
- 2 tablespoons Chinese rice wine
- 1/2 teaspoon sesame oil
- 1 tablespoon thinly sliced fresh ginger
- 4 x 200 g (6 1/2 oz) chicken breast fillets, trimmed
- 450 g (14 oz) bok choy, ends removed and cut lengthways into quarters
- 1/2 cup (125 ml/4 fl oz) chicken stock
- 1 tablespoon cornflour

preparation: 10 minutes + 20 minutes soaking + 1 hour marinating
cooking: 20 minutes
serves: 4

1 Soak the mushrooms in 1/4 cup (60 ml/2 fl oz) boiling water for 20 minutes. Drain, reserving the soaking liquid. Discard the stalks and thinly slice the caps.

2 Combine the soy sauce, rice wine, sesame oil and ginger in a non-metallic dish. Add the chicken to the marinade and turn so that it is well coated. Cover and marinate in the fridge for 1 hour.

3 Line a bamboo steamer with baking paper. Remove the chicken from the marinade, reserving the liquid. Place the chicken in the steamer. Bring water to the boil in a wok, then place the steamer over the wok. Cover and steam for 6 minutes, then turn the chicken over and steam for a further 6 minutes. Place the bok choy on top of the chicken and steam for a further 2–3 minutes.

4 Meanwhile, place the reserved marinade, mushrooms and their soaking liquid in a small saucepan and bring to the boil. Add enough stock to the cornflour in a small bowl to make a smooth paste. Add the cornflour paste and remaining stock to the pan and stir over medium heat for 2 minutes, or until the sauce thickens.

5 Place some bok choy and a chicken fillet on each plate, then pour on some sauce. Serve with steamed rice.

nutrition per serve
Fat 5.5 g; Protein 45.5 g; Carbohydrate 4.5 g; Dietary Fibre 2 g; Cholesterol 95 mg; 1085 kJ (260 Cal)

cooking hint

To test whether the chicken breast is cooked, press it with your finger. If it feels slightly springy to the touch, the chicken is cooked.

chicken wrapped in vine leaves

ingredients

- 4 x 180 g (6 oz) single chicken breast fillets
- 8–12 vine leaves packed in brine, rinsed and patted dry
- 2 eggs
- ¼ cup (60 ml/2 fl oz) lemon juice
- 1 cup (250 ml/8 fl oz) chicken stock
- 1 tablespoon chopped fresh dill

preparation: 15 minutes
cooking: 25 minutes
serves: 4

1 Preheat the oven to moderately hot 200°C (400°F/Gas 6). Season each chicken breast with salt and freshly ground black pepper. Wrap each breast in 2–3 vine leaves (the number will vary depending on the size of the leaves), then in baking paper and, finally, in foil. Bake for 20 minutes.

2 While the chicken is cooking, make the avgolemono sauce. Crack the eggs into a bowl and whisk until they are frothy. Slowly pour in the lemon juice and mix gently. Heat the chicken stock in a small saucepan. Gradually whisk the hot stock into the eggs. When it is completely incorporated, return the mixture to the saucepan and whisk over medium–low heat until the mixture has thickened, being careful not to allow the mixture to boil or the eggs will scramble. Stir in the chopped dill and remove the pan from the heat.

3 Carefully remove the foil and baking paper from the chicken, transfer the chicken to four serving plates and drizzle with the sauce. Serve immediately.

nutrition per serve
Fat 7 g; Protein 45.5 g; Carbohydrate 1 g; Dietary Fibre 1 g; Cholesterol 180 mg; 1050 kJ (250 Cal)

cooking hint

It is important to thoroughly rinse the vine leaves in warm water and pat them dry with paper towel to remove the excess brine.

chicken cacciatore with feta and black olives

ingredients

- 2 tablespoons oil
- 1.2 kg chicken pieces, with skin on
- 1 onion, chopped
- 25 g (3/4 oz) fresh oregano, leaves picked
- 2 tablespoons tomato paste
- 2 x 425 g (14 oz) cans chopped tomatoes
- 150 g (5 oz) black olives
- 150 g (5 oz) feta, crumbled

preparation: 15 minutes
cooking: 1 hour
serves: 4

1 Heat half the oil in a saucepan and cook the chicken pieces in batches for 3–4 minutes, or until they are golden brown. Remove the chicken from the pan with tongs and set aside.

2 In the same saucepan, heat the remaining oil and cook the onion and half the oregano for 3 minutes, or until the onion is soft. Add the tomato paste to the onion mixture and stir for 2 minutes before adding the chopped tomato and chicken pieces.

3 Put the lid on the pan and simmer for 40–50 minutes, or until the chicken is cooked through. Add the olives and remaining oregano leaves. To serve, spoon into bowls and top with the crumbled feta.

nutrition per serve
Fat 28 g; Protein 50 g; Carbohydrate 11 g; Dietary Fibre 5 g; Cholesterol 165 mg; 2110 kJ (505 Cal)

shopping tip

Buy chicken pieces that are still on the bone. The bone will help the chicken flesh remain moist and succulent during cooking.

chicken and snow pea sprouts stir-fry

ingredients

- 2 tablespoons oil
- 1 onion, thinly sliced
- 3 fresh kaffir lime leaves, finely shredded
- 3 chicken breast fillets, cut into 2 cm (3/4 inch) cubes
- 1 red capsicum, sliced
- 1/4 cup (60 ml/2 fl oz) lime juice
- 100 ml soy sauce
- 100 g (3 1/2 oz) snow pea sprouts
- 2 tablespoons chopped fresh coriander leaves

preparation: 15 minutes
cooking: 15 minutes
serves: 4

1 Heat a wok or large frying pan over medium heat, add the oil and swirl to coat. Add the onion and kaffir lime leaves and stir-fry for 3–5 minutes, or until the onion begins to soften. Add the chicken and cook for a further 4 minutes. Add the capsicum and continue to cook for 2–3 minutes.

2 Stir in the lime juice and soy sauce and cook for 1–2 minutes, or until the sauce reduces a little. Add the sprouts and coriander and cook until the sprouts have wilted slightly. Serve with some steamed jasmine rice and extra coriander and chilli, if desired.

nutrition per serve
Fat 15 g; Protein 45 g; Carbohydrate 5.5 g; Dietary Fibre 2 g; Cholesterol 90 mg; 1375 kJ (330 Cal)

variation

Use the chicken, soy sauce and lime juice as a base for the stir-fry and add or subtract ingredients to your taste. For example, add fresh asparagus, a touch of fresh chilli or basil.

parsley and parmesan crumbed chicken

ingredients

4 chicken breast fillets
plain flour, to coat
3/4 cup (75 g/2 1/2 oz) dry breadcrumbs
1/2 cup (50 g/1 3/4 oz) grated Parmesan
1/2 cup (15 g/1/2 oz) chopped fresh flat-leaf parsley
1 egg, lightly beaten
2 tablespoons milk
1/4 cup (60 ml/2 fl oz) oil

preparation: 15 minutes + 30 minutes refrigeration
cooking: 30 minutes
serves: 4

1 Lay the chicken breast fillets out between two sheets of plastic wrap and flatten them by beating them gently with a meat mallet or rolling pin. Evenly coat the fillets in the plain flour.

2 Put the breadcrumbs, Parmesan and parsley in a wide, shallow bowl and mix together well. Combine the egg and milk in a separate bowl. Coat the chicken fillets by dipping them first into the egg, and then into the crumb mixture. Press the crumb mixture firmly onto the chicken and leave in the fridge for 30 minutes to ensure that the crumbs adhere to the chicken.

3 Heat the oil in a frying pan over medium heat. Add two of the chicken breasts and cook, turning once only, for 10–15 minutes, or until the chicken is cooked through. Set aside in a warm place, then repeat with the remaining chicken breast fillets. Serve with lemon wedges and boiled new potatoes, drizzled with a little melted butter and fresh chives.

nutrition per serve
Fat 23 g; Protein 35 g; Carbohydrate 17 g; Dietary Fibre 1 g; Cholesterol 118 mg; 1782 kJ (425 Cal)

think ahead

The crumbed chicken breasts can be prepared ahead and kept in the refrigerator overnight or sealed well in plastic and frozen.

baked chicken and leek risotto

ingredients

60 g (2 oz) butter
1 leek, thinly sliced
2 chicken breast fillets, cut into 2 cm (3/4 inch) cubes
2 cups (440 g/14 oz) arborio rice
1/4 cup (60 ml/2 fl oz) dry white wine
1.25 litres chicken stock
1/3 cup (35 g/1 1/4 oz) grated Parmesan
2 tablespoons fresh thyme
fresh thyme, to garnish
grated Parmesan, extra

preparation: 10 minutes
cooking: 40 minutes
serves: 4–6

1 Preheat the oven to slow 150°C (300°F/Gas 2) and place a 5 litre ovenproof dish with a lid in the oven to warm. Heat the butter in a saucepan over medium heat, add the leek and cook for 2 minutes, or until soft.

2 Add the chicken and cook, stirring, for 2–3 minutes, or until it colours. Add the rice and stir so that it is well coated with butter. Cook for 1 minute.

3 Add the wine and stock and bring to the boil. Pour the mixture into the warm ovenproof dish and cover. Place in the oven and cook for 30 minutes, stirring halfway through. Remove from the oven and stir through the Parmesan and thyme leaves. Season to taste. Sprinkle with extra thyme leaves and extra Parmesan, and serve.

nutrition per serve (6)
Fat 15 g; Protein 28 g; Carbohydrate 60 g; Dietary Fibre 3 g; Cholesterol 75 mg; 2014 kJ (480 Cal)

shopping tip

Arborio rice is a special short-grain rice valued for use in risottos because its high starch content gives the risotto its classic creaminess. It is readily available in most supermarkets.

vietnamese chicken salad

ingredients

1 small Chinese cabbage, finely shredded
2 tablespoons oil
2 onions, thinly sliced
500 g (1 lb) chicken thigh fillets, trimmed and cut into strips
1/4 cup (60 g/2 oz) sugar
1/4 cup (60 ml/2 fl oz) fish sauce
1/3 cup (80 ml/2 3/4 fl oz) lime juice
1 tablespoon white vinegar
2/3 cup (30 g/1 oz) chopped fresh Vietnamese mint or mint, plus extra, to garnish
2/3 cup (30 g/1 oz) chopped fresh coriander

preparation: 15 minutes
cooking: 10 minutes
serves: 6

1 Put the shredded cabbage in a large bowl, cover with plastic wrap and refrigerate until needed.

2 Heat a wok until very hot, add 1 tablespoon of the oil and swirl to coat the side of the wok. Add half the sliced onion and half the chicken, and stir-fry for about 5 minutes, or until the chicken is cooked. Remove from the wok and set aside. Reheat the wok to hot and repeat with the remaining oil, onion and chicken. Cool.

3 To make the dressing, put the sugar, fish sauce, lime juice, vinegar and 1/2 teaspoon salt in a small jug, and mix well until the sugar and salt have dissolved. To serve, toss together the cabbage, chicken and onion, dressing, mint and coriander, and garnish with the extra mint leaves.

nutrition per serve
Fat 8 g; Protein 17 g; Carbohydrate 13 g; Dietary Fibre 1.5 g; Cholesterol 35 mg; 805 kJ (190 Cal)

serving tip

This is delicious served with prawn crackers to scoop up the salad.
Dress the salad just before you are ready to eat it so that it doesn't go soggy.

chicken and lemon grass stir-fry

ingredients

1 tablespoon fish sauce
3 teaspoons grated palm sugar
1 tablespoon peanut oil
2 teaspoons sesame oil
800 g (1 lb 10 oz) chicken breast fillets, cut into strips
2 tablespoons finely chopped lemon grass, white part only
1½ tablespoons julienned fresh ginger
2 cloves garlic, finely chopped
2 tablespoons fresh coriander leaves
2 limes, cut into wedges

preparation: 15 minutes
cooking: 15 minutes
serves: 4

1 Place the fish sauce and palm sugar in a small bowl and stir until all the sugar has dissolved.

2 Heat a large wok until very hot, add half the combined peanut and sesame oils and swirl to coat. Add half the chicken and stir-fry for 4 minutes, then remove from the wok. Add the lemon grass, ginger and garlic to the wok, and stir-fry for 1–2 minutes, then return all the chicken to the wok and stir-fry for 2 minutes more.

3 Stir in the combined fish sauce and palm sugar. Scatter with the coriander and serve immediately with noodles or steamed rice, and the lime wedges.

nutrition per serve
Fat 15 g; Protein 45 g; Carbohydrate 2 g; Dietary fibre 0 g; Cholesterol 100 mg; 1330 kJ (318 Cal)

cooking hint

If you want to add a kick to your stir-fry, add 1–2 seeded and finely chopped fresh bird's eye chillies to the pan when adding the lemon grass, ginger and garlic. Wear gloves when chopping the chilli.

22 chargrilled chicken with salsa verde

ingredients

- 1 clove garlic
- 2 cups (60 g/2 oz) firmly packed fresh flat-leaf parsley
- 1/3 cup (80 ml/2 3/4 fl oz) extra virgin olive oil
- 3 tablespoons chopped fresh dill
- 1 1/2 tablespoons Dijon mustard
- 1 tablespoon sherry vinegar
- 1 tablespoon baby capers, drained
- 6 large chicken breast fillets

preparation: 10 minutes
cooking: 10 minutes
serves: 6

1 To make the salsa verde, place the garlic, parsley, oil, dill, mustard, sherry vinegar and baby capers in a food processor or blender and process until the mixture is combined and almost smooth. Season to taste with salt and freshly ground black pepper.

2 Lightly grease a barbecue or chargrill pan and heat to very hot. Cook the chicken fillets for about 5 minutes on each side, or until cooked through.

3 Cut each chicken fillet into three slices on the diagonal and arrange on six serving plates. Top with a spoonful of the salsa verde. Serve with a fresh green salad or lightly steamed vegetables.

nutrition per serve
Fat 18 g; Protein 50 g; Carbohydrate 0 g; Dietary Fibre 0.5 g; Cholesterol 110 mg; 1510 kJ (360 Cal)

storage hint

If you have any leftover salsa verde, spoon it into a small bowl and place a piece of plastic wrap directly onto the surface of the salsa to help prevent any discolouration. It will keep in the refrigerator for up to 3 days.

chicken with prosciutto and white wine mushroom sauce

ingredients

- 60 g (2 oz) butter
- 4 chicken breast fillets
- 2 thin slices prosciutto
- 1 clove garlic, crushed
- 200 g (6½ oz) button mushrooms, sliced
- ⅔ cup (170 ml/5½ fl oz) dry white wine
- 2–3 tablespoons chopped fresh tarragon
- ½ cup (110 g/3½ oz) mascarpone

preparation: 5 minutes
cooking: 20 minutes
serves: 4

1 Melt half the butter in a frying pan, add the chicken and cook over medium heat for 3–4 minutes on each side, or until golden brown and cooked through. Transfer to a warm serving dish. Cut the prosciutto in half widthways and place half a slice over each chicken fillet. Cover the serving dish with foil and keep warm.

2 Melt the remaining butter in the frying pan, add the garlic and mushrooms, and cook, stirring, over medium heat for 2–3 minutes, or until the mushrooms are soft. Add the wine and most of the tarragon, bring to the boil and cook over high heat for 5 minutes, or until the wine is reduced by half.

3 Stir in the mascarpone and heat gently until warmed through. Do not boil or it will split. Season to taste with salt and freshly ground black pepper and spoon the sauce over the chicken. Garnish with the remaining tarragon, and serve with steamed vegetables.

nutrition per serve
Fat 24 g; Protein 30 g; Carbohydrate 2 g; Dietary Fibre 1.5 g; Cholesterol 122 mg; 1544 kJ (370 Cal)

shopping tip

Mascarpone is a rich, creamy soft cheese made from cow's milk. It is available from most delicatessens and some large supermarkets. If you can't find mascarpone, use sour cream or crème fraîche instead.

26 delicious sauces for chicken breast fillets

PAN-FRIED CHICKEN BREASTS

Trim 4 x 200 g (6½ oz) skinless chicken breast fillets (tenderloins removed) of any excess fat and sinew, then season them lightly with salt and freshly ground black pepper. Heat a heavy-based frying pan over medium heat, add 40 g (1¼ oz) butter and 1 tablespoon oil and when it is hot, but not burning, add the chicken breasts and cook for 2–3 minutes on each side, or until golden and cooked through. The chicken is done when just springy to the touch. Transfer to warm plates and leave to rest for 5–6 minutes, or while making the sauce, before serving.

serves 4

mushroom sauce

Leave the fat from cooking the chicken in the pan and add 20 g (¾ oz) butter. When the butter begins to foam, add 350 g (11 oz) thinly sliced button mushrooms and cook over high heat for 5–6 minutes, tossing the pan constantly, until the mushrooms are lightly browned. Add a little more butter if it seems too dry, then add 2 cloves crushed garlic and 2 teaspoons chopped fresh thyme and cook for 1 more minute. Add 75 ml (2½ fl oz) dry white wine to the pan, and cook until it has nearly all evaporated, then add ½ cup (125 ml/4 fl oz) chicken stock and ¾ cup (185 ml/6 fl oz) cream. Bring to the boil, reduce the heat and simmer for 5–6 minutes, or until the sauce has thickened and reduced. Season to taste, then drizzle over the chicken and serve.

lemon and basil sauce

Drain off any excess fat from the frying pan, then add 100 g (3½ oz) butter. Cook over medium heat until the butter turns a light hazelnut colour, then add 2 tablespoons lemon juice and 4 tablespoons torn fresh basil. Season lightly with salt and freshly ground black pepper, and serve drizzled over the chicken breasts.

Note: Don't make this sauce ahead of time, or the basil will turn brown.

marsala sauce

Drain off any excess fat from the frying pan, then add ½ cup (125 ml/4 fl oz) dry Marsala and cook over medium heat for 1–2 minutes, using a wooden spoon to scrape up any sediment from the bottom of the pan. Pour in ½ cup (125 ml/4 fl oz) chicken stock and ⅓ cup (80 ml/2¾ fl oz) cream. Bring to the boil, reduce the heat and simmer for 5–6 minutes, or until thickened and reduced. Strain the sauce to remove any sediment. Drizzle over the chicken breasts and serve.

tarragon and mustard sauce

Drain off any excess fat from the frying pan, then add 20 g (¾ oz) butter and cook 4 thinly sliced French shallots over low heat until soft but not browned. Add 100 ml (3½ fl oz) dry white wine to the pan and cook over medium heat until nearly all the wine has evaporated. Pour in 200 ml (6½ fl oz) each of chicken stock and cream and simmer for 6–8 minutes, or until the sauce has reduced and thickened. Stir in 2 tablespoons Dijon mustard and 1 tablespoon chopped fresh tarragon and cook for a further 2–3 minutes. Season to taste, then drizzle over the chicken breasts, and serve.

cooking hint

Each of the sauces takes a different time to cook and needs to be started at a different time. Prepare the Lemon and basil sauce and Marsala sauce while the chicken is resting, but start the other two while the chicken is cooking.

From left to right: Mushroom sauce, Lemon and basil sauce, Marsala sauce, Tarragon and mushroom sauce.

smoked chicken and spinach stir-fry

ingredients

- 300 g (10 oz) smoked chicken breast
- 1 tablespoon olive oil
- 100 g (3½ oz) marinated chargrilled capsicum, cut into thin strips
- ⅓ cup (50 g/1¾ oz) pine nuts
- 500 g (1 lb) English spinach, trimmed
- 1 tablespoon light sour cream
- 2 teaspoons wholegrain mustard
- 3 tablespoons fresh basil, finely shredded

preparation: 10 minutes
cooking: 10 minutes
serves: 4

1 Cut the smoked chicken breast into even-sized thin strips with a sharp knife.

2 Heat a wok or large frying pan over high heat, add the oil and swirl it around to coat the side of the wok or pan. Add the chicken and capsicum strips and the pine nuts and stir-fry for 3–4 minutes, or until the nuts are golden brown. Add the English spinach leaves and stir-fry for 2–3 minutes, or until the leaves have wilted.

3 Stir in the sour cream, mustard and shredded basil until well combined. Season to taste with some salt and freshly ground black pepper and serve with boiled noodles or rice.

nutrition per serve
Fat 13 g; Protein 22 g; Carbohydrate 2.5 g; Dietary Fibre 4.5 g; Cholesterol 45 mg; 900 kJ (215 Cal)

cooking hint

To make your own chargrilled capsicum, cut capsicums into large pieces, removing the seeds and membrane. Place, skin-side-up, under a hot grill until the skin blackens and blisters. Transfer to a bowl, cover with plastic wrap and allow to cool. Peel away the skin, then cut the flesh into thin strips.

Ingredients

- 30 g (1 oz) butter
- 1 onion, thinly sliced
- 2 cloves garlic, crushed
- 600 g ($1^{1}/_{4}$ lb) chicken tenderloins
- 2 cups (180 g/6 oz) sliced button mushrooms
- $^{1}/_{4}$ cup (60 g/2 oz) tomato paste
- 300 g (10 oz) sour cream

preparation: 15 minutes
cooking: 25 minutes
serves: 4

1 Melt half the butter in a frying pan, add the onion and cook for 5 minutes, or until soft. Add the garlic and cook for 1 minute, then remove. Melt the remaining butter over high heat and brown the chicken in batches. Set aside with the garlic and onion mixture. In the same pan, brown the mushrooms for 1–2 minutes.

2 Return the onion mixture and chicken to the pan. Remove from the heat and stir in the tomato paste and sour cream. Return to the heat and cook, stirring constantly, until the mixture thickens. Reduce the heat and simmer for 5 minutes, or until the chicken is cooked through. Season to taste with salt and freshly ground black pepper. Serve with pasta and steamed green beans and asparagus.

nutrition per serve

Fat 40 g; Protein 40 g; Carbohydrate 7.5 g; Dietary Fibre 2.5 g; Cholesterol 190 mg; 2255 kJ (540 Cal)

cooking hint

If the chicken tenderloins are very large, cut them in half lengthways on the diagonal. If you are serving this with pasta, try using 250 g (8 oz) farfalle and stir through a little butter once cooked.

30 satay chicken stir-fry

ingredients

- 1½ cups (300 g/10 oz) jasmine rice
- 1½ tablespoons peanut oil
- 6 spring onions, cut into 3 cm (1¼ inch) lengths
- 800 g (1 lb 10 oz) chicken breast fillets, thinly sliced
- 1–1½ tablespoons ready-made Thai red curry paste
- ⅓ cup (90 g/3 oz) crunchy peanut butter
- 270 ml (9 fl oz) coconut milk
- 2 teaspoons soft brown sugar
- 1½ tablespoons lime juice

preparation: 10 minutes
cooking: 20 minutes
serves: 4

1 Bring a large saucepan of water to the boil. Add the jasmine rice and cook for 12 minutes, stirring occasionally. Drain well.

2 Meanwhile, heat a wok until very hot, add 1 teaspoon of the peanut oil and swirl to coat. When smoking, add the spring onion and stir-fry for 30 seconds, or until softened slightly. Remove from the wok. Add a little extra peanut oil to the wok as needed and stir-fry the chicken in three batches for about 1 minute per batch, or until the meat just changes colour. Remove from the wok.

3 Add a little more oil to the wok, add the curry paste and stir-fry for 1 minute, or until fragrant. Add the peanut butter, coconut milk, sugar and 1 cup (250 ml/8 fl oz) water and stir well. Bring to the boil and boil for 3–4 minutes, or until thickened and the oil starts to separate—reduce the heat slightly if the sauce spits. Return the chicken and spring onion to the wok, stir and cook for 2 minutes, or until heated through. Stir in the lime juice and season well. Serve at once with the rice and a crisp green salad.

nutrition per serve
Fat 46 g; Protein 55 g; Carbohydrate 57.5 g; Dietary Fibre 5.5 g; Cholesterol 132 mg; 3600 kJ (860 Cal)

cooking hint

If you want an added kick to your stir-fry, garnish with 2 thinly sliced, seeded fresh bird's eye chillies. They are very hot, so protect your hands by wearing plastic gloves when you slice them.

mexican chicken bake

ingredients

- 3/4 cup (165 g/5 1/2 oz) short-grain rice
- 300 g (10 oz) can red kidney beans, drained and thoroughly rinsed
- 3 1/2 tablespoons chopped fresh coriander leaves
- 1 tablespoon oil
- 600 g (1 1/4 lb) boneless, skinless chicken thigh fillets, unrolled and cut in half
- 2 x 200 g (6 1/2 oz) jars spicy taco sauce
- 2 cups (250 g/8 oz) grated Cheddar
- 1/2 cup (125 g/4 oz) sour cream

preparation: 15 minutes
cooking: 1 hour
serves: 4

1 Preheat the oven to moderate 180°C (350°F/Gas 4). Lightly grease a deep 1.75 litre round ceramic casserole dish. Bring a large saucepan of water to the boil, add the rice and cook for 10–12 minutes stirring occasionally. Drain.

2 In the prepared dish, combine the beans and 1 1/2 tablespoons of the coriander, then add the rice and toss together. Lightly press the mixture so the beans are slightly covered and the mixture is flat.

3 Heat the oil in a large frying pan over medium–high heat. Sauté the chicken thighs for 3 minutes, then turn over. Add the spicy taco sauce, and cook for a further 3 minutes.

4 To assemble, spread half the cheese over the rice. Arrange the chicken thighs on top in a star shape with the sauce, sprinkle with 1 1/2 tablespoons of the coriander, then sprinkle with the remaining cheese. Cover.

5 Bake for 35–40 minutes, or until the mixture is bubbling and the cheese is melted and slightly browned. Cut into four servings with a knife and scoop out carefully. Sprinkle with the remaining coriander and a dollop of sour cream and serve.

nutrition per serve
Fat 49.5 g; Protein 52 g; Carbohydrate 66 g; Dietary Fibre 6 g; Cholesterol 234.5 mg; 2825 kJ (915 Cal)

variation

This dish will work just as well using beef instead of chicken: substitute the chicken with 500 g (1 lb) beef mince. Cook the mince over medium heat for 4–5 minutes, breaking up any lumps with the back of a wooden spoon, before adding the taco sauce.

thai green chicken curry

ingredients

- $1\frac{1}{4}$ cups (250 g/8 oz) jasmine rice
- 1 tablespoon oil
- 2 tablespoons ready-made Thai green curry paste
- 4 fresh kaffir lime leaves
- 1 tablespoon fish sauce
- 2 teaspoons grated palm sugar
- 400 ml (13 fl oz) can coconut cream
- 750 g ($1\frac{1}{2}$ lb) skinless chicken breasts, cut into strips
- 4 tablespoons roughly chopped fresh coriander leaves, plus whole leaves, to garnish

preparation: 10 minutes
cooking: 20 minutes
serves: 4

1 Bring a large saucepan of water to the boil. Add the jasmine rice and cook for 12 minutes, stirring occasionally. Drain well.

2 Meanwhile, heat a wok over high heat, add the oil and swirl to coat. Reduce the heat to medium, add the curry paste and lime leaves and stir-fry for 1–2 minutes, or until fragrant. Add the fish sauce and palm sugar and mix. Pour in the coconut cream, bring to the boil, then add the chicken. Reduce the heat to medium and simmer for 12–15 minutes, or until the sauce is reduced and the chicken is tender and cooked through.

3 Just before serving, stir the chopped coriander through the rice. Serve the curry over the rice, then garnish with coriander leaves.

nutrition per serve
Fat 38.5 g; Protein 47 g; Carbohydrate 56 g; Dietary Fibre 3.5 g; Cholesterol 124 mg; 3170 kJ (760 Cal)

shopping tip

Palm sugar is a rich, aromatic sugar made from the sap of sugar palm trees. It is available in block form in Asian food stores. If you can't find palm sugar, you can substitute soft brown sugar.

individual chicken and leek pies

ingredients

- 875 ml (28 fl oz) chicken and herb stock
- 4 x 200 g (6½ oz) chicken breasts
- 60 g (2 oz) butter
- 1 leek, thinly sliced
- 50 g (1¾ oz) plain flour
- 300 ml (9½ fl oz) cream
- 1 cup (155 g/5 oz) fresh or frozen peas, blanched
- 1 sheet ready-rolled puff pastry

preparation: 15 minutes + cooling
cooking: 1 hour
serves: 4

1 Place the stock in a deep-sided frying pan, then bring to the boil. Reduce the heat to medium–low so that the liquid is just simmering, then gently poach the chicken for 10–12 minutes (if necessary, add 100 ml (3½ fl oz) water to keep the chicken covered). Allow to cool in the liquid. Remove the chicken, reserving the liquid, and cut into bite-sized pieces.

2 Preheat the oven to moderately hot 200°C (400°F/Gas 6). Melt the butter in a saucepan over medium heat and cook the leek for 5 minutes, or until soft. Add the flour and cook, stirring, until it starts to bubble. Pour in 1 cup (250 ml/8 fl oz) of the reserved liquid and continue to cook until it starts to thicken. Add the cream, reserving 1 tablespoon to glaze the pastry. Cook until the mixture just starts to boil. Stir in the chicken and the peas and continue to cook for 5–6 minutes. Season well. Remove from the heat and cool.

3 Divide the filling among four individual pie or ramekin dishes. Top with a circle of pastry, cut just bigger than the top of the dish, then brush with the reserved cream. Place the dishes on a metal tray and bake for 20–25 minutes, or until the golden. Serve with a salad.

nutrition per serve
Fat 65.5 g; Protein 53 g; Carbohydrate 30.5 g; Dietary Fibre 3.5 g; Cholesterol 284 mg; 3835 kJ (915 Cal)

variation

To make one large pie, transfer the filling to a 20 cm (8 inch) ceramic pie dish or 1.5 litre ovenproof dish. Press the pastry sheet over the filling, then trim to fit.

CHICKEN STIR-FRY

Cut 600 g (1¼ lb) chicken thigh fillets in half lengthways, then across the grain into six pieces. Mix 1 tablespoon soy sauce, ½ teaspoon sesame oil, 2 cloves crushed garlic and 1 teaspoon grated fresh ginger in a non-metallic bowl. Add the chicken and stir to coat well. Cover with plastic wrap and marinate in the fridge for 2 hours.

Make your stir-fry sauce from the adjacent recipes. Heat a wok over high heat, add 1 teaspoon sesame oil and 1 tablespoon peanut oil and swirl to coat. When hot, add the chicken in batches and stir-fry until the chicken is just cooked through. Add a little more oil if needed. Remove from the wok.

Heat another tablespoon of peanut oil in the wok, add 400 g (13 oz) mixed vegetables (e.g. bok choy, baby corn, snow peas or oyster mushrooms) and stir-fry for 3 minutes. Add your prepared stir-fry sauce and the chicken with any juices. Stir well and cook for 3 minutes, or until the sauce has thickened enough to lightly coat the chicken and vegetables. Remove from the heat, season to taste with salt and freshly ground black pepper, and serve with steamed rice.

serves 4

basic stir-fry sauce

Combine ¼ cup (60 ml/2 fl oz) oyster sauce, ¼ cup (60 ml/2 fl oz) chicken stock, 2 teaspoons soy sauce and 1 teaspoon cornflour in a small bowl. Add to the stir-fry when you return the cooked chicken to the wok.

plum and ginger sauce

Combine ½ cup (125 ml/4 fl oz) plum sauce, 2 teaspoons grated fresh ginger, ¼ cup (60 ml/2 fl oz) chicken stock, 2 teaspoons rice vinegar and ¼ teaspoon cornflour in a small bowl. Add to the stir-fry when you return the cooked chicken to the wok.

Lime, chilli and basil sauce

In a small bowl, combine 1/4 cup (60 ml/2 fl oz) lime juice, 1–2 finely chopped small fresh red chillies, 1 1/2 tablespoons fish sauce, 1 teaspoon grated palm sugar or soft brown sugar and 1 teaspoon cornflour. Mix well. Add to the stir-fry when you return the cooked chicken to the wok and toss for 3 minutes, or until the mixture has thickened enough to coat all the ingredients. Remove the wok from the heat, then add 4 tablespoons torn fresh basil and briefly stir through.

sesame, soy and honey sauce

In a small bowl, mix together 3 teaspoons honey, 1 1/2 teaspoons sesame oil, 2 tablespoons toasted sesame seeds, 1 teaspoon cornflour and 1/4 cup (60 ml/2 fl oz) each of soy sauce and chicken stock. Add to the stir-fry when you add the cooked chicken.

From left to right: Basic sauce, Plum and ginger sauce, Lime, chilli and basil sauce, Sesame, soy and honey sauce.

variation

Add 4 tablespoons fresh coriander leaves and 2 thinly sliced spring onions to any of the stir-fry sauces just before serving.

chicken provençale

ingredients

- 1 tablespoon olive oil
- 1.5 kg (3 lb) chicken pieces
- 1 onion, chopped
- 1 red capsicum, chopped
- 1/3 cup (80 ml/2 3/4 fl oz) dry white wine
- 1/3 cup (80 ml/2 3/4 fl oz) chicken stock
- 425 g (14 oz) can chopped tomatoes
- 2 tablespoons tomato paste
- 1/2 cup (90 g/3 oz) black olives
- 4 tablespoons shredded fresh basil

preparation: 15 minutes
cooking: 1 hour 20 minutes
serves: 4–6

1 Heat the oil in a saucepan over high heat, add the chicken pieces in batches and cook each batch for about 3 minutes, or until nicely browned all over. Return all the chicken to the pan and add the onion and capsicum. Cook for 2–3 minutes, or until the onion has softened.

2 Pour in the wine and stock, then add the chopped tomatoes and tomato paste and bring to the boil. Reduce the heat to low, cover with a lid and simmer for 30 minutes.

3 Remove the lid, turn the chicken pieces over with tongs, stir in the olives and cook for a further 30 minutes, or until the chicken is tender and the cooking liquid has thickened. Season to taste with salt, freshly ground black pepper and a little sugar, if desired. Sprinkle with some shredded fresh basil and serve with steamed rice or pasta.

nutrition per serve (6)
Fat 10 g; Protein 35 g; Carbohydrate 5 g; Dietary Fibre 2 g; Cholesterol 115 mg; 1133 kJ (270 Cal)

shopping tip

Buy chicken pieces such as thighs or drumsticks for this dish because they stay moister and more succulent during cooking than chicken breasts.

chicken meatballs

ingredients

500 g (1 lb) chicken mince
1/4 cup (20 g/3/4 oz) fresh breadcrumbs
2 teaspoons finely chopped fresh thyme
2 tablespoons oil
1 onion, finely chopped
2 x 425 g (14 oz) cans chopped tomatoes
2 teaspoons balsamic vinegar
1 cup (250 ml/8 fl oz) chicken stock

preparation: 15 minutes
cooking: 30 minutes
serves: 4–6

1 Combine the chicken mince, breadcrumbs and thyme in a large bowl and season with salt and pepper. Roll a tablespoon of the mixture between your hands to make a meatball, and then repeat with the remaining mixture.

2 Heat the oil in a large frying pan and cook the meatballs in batches for 5–8 minutes, or until golden brown. Remove from the pan and drain on crumpled paper towels.

3 Add the onion to the pan and cook for 2–3 minutes, or until softened. Add the tomato, vinegar and stock, return the meatballs to the pan, then reduce the heat and simmer for 10 minutes, or until the sauce thickens and the meatballs are cooked through. Serve with pasta and garnish with finely shredded fresh basil and freshly grated Parmesan, if desired.

nutrition per serve (6)
Fat 8.5 g; Protein 20 g; Carbohydrate 7.5 g; Dietary Fibre 2 g; Cholesterol 42 mg; 812 kJ (194 Cal)

cooking hint

Use the meatball recipe as a starting point and try adding different spices, such as cayenne pepper, ground cumin or ground coriander.

42 chicken with goat's cheese and couscous

ingredients

4 chicken breast fillets
150 g (5 oz) goat's cheese, roughly chopped
150 g (5 oz) semi-dried tomatoes, finely chopped
3 tablespoons shredded fresh basil
1 cup (185 g/6 oz) couscous
1 tablespoon lemon juice
1 tablespoon olive oil
lemon wedges, to serve

preparation: 15 minutes + 5 minutes standing
cooking: 20 minutes
serves: 4

1 Cut a pocket lengthways into the thickest part of each chicken breast, being careful not to cut all the way through. Put the goat's cheese, tomato and 2 tablespoons of the basil in a small bowl and mix well. Divide the mixture into four and press into the chicken breast pockets. Secure the opening with a few toothpicks.

2 Heat the oil in a large non-stick frying pan, add the chicken breasts and cook over medium heat for 8–10 minutes on each side, or until golden and cooked through. Carefully cut the chicken into slices on the diagonal.

3 Meanwhile, place the couscous in a heatproof bowl. Cover with the lemon juice and 1 cup (250 ml/ 8 fl oz) boiling water. Stand for 5 minutes, then fluff with a fork and fold in the remaining basil. To serve, place the chicken slices on a bed of couscous with the lemon wedges on the side.

nutrition per serve
Fat 20 g; Protein 60 g; Carbohydrate 33 g; Dietary Fibre 2 g; Cholesterol 136 mg; 2311 kJ (552 Cal)

variation

For a richer-flavoured couscous, you can replace the boiling water with boiling chicken stock and stir through 20 g (3/4 oz) butter when adding the remaining basil.

ingredients

- 1/4 cup (60 ml/2 fl oz) light olive oil
- 10 chicken thigh fillets, cut into small pieces
- 3 teaspoons grated fresh ginger
- 1 teaspoon grated orange rind
- 1/2 cup (125 ml/4 fl oz) chicken stock
- 2 teaspoons honey
- 550 g (1lb 3/4 oz) bok choy, trimmed and halved
- toasted sesame seeds, to garnish

preparation: 15 minutes
cooking: 20 minutes
serves: 4

1 Heat a wok or large frying pan over high heat, add the oil and swirl to coat. Add the chicken pieces in batches and stir-fry each batch for 3–4 minutes, or until golden.

2 Return all the chicken pieces to the wok or pan, add the ginger and orange rind, and cook for about 20 seconds, or until fragrant. Add the stock and the honey, stir well until combined and cook for 3–4 minutes, or until the sauce has thickened slightly. Add the bok choy and cook until slightly wilted. Season with salt and black pepper. Sprinkle with toasted sesame seeds and serve with steamed rice.

nutrition per serve
Fat 20 g; Protein 70 g Carbohydrate 3.5 g; Dietary Fibre 0.5 g; Cholesterol 150 mg; 2005 kJ (480 Cal)

cooking hint

The oil in the wok should always just begin to smoke before you add any meat. This will ensure that the wok is hot enough to prevent the meat from stewing and becoming dry.

chicken tandoori pizza

ingredients

1 cup (250 g/8 oz) plain yoghurt
2 tablespoons tandoori paste
3 chicken breasts
1 cup (250 g/8 oz) tomato paste
2 cloves garlic, crushed
2 teaspoons ground cumin
2 x 28 cm (11 inch) round ready-made pizza bases
1/4 cup (70 g/2 1/4 oz) mango chutney
2/3 cup (160 g/5 1/2 oz) yoghurt, extra
1/2 cup (25 g/3/4 oz) roughly chopped fresh coriander leaves
snow pea sprouts, to garnish

preparation: 15 minutes + 30 minutes marinating
cooking: 30 minutes
serves: 4

1 Combine the yoghurt and tandoori paste in a large bowl. Add the chicken breasts and cover them in the marinade. Cover and refrigerate for 30 minutes.

2 Cook the chicken on a lightly oiled preheated grill for about 4 minutes on each side, or until browned but not cooked through. Slice the chicken into strips on the diagonal.

3 Combine the tomato paste, garlic and cumin. Spread the pizza bases with the tomato mix, leaving a 1 cm (1/2 inch) border. Sprinkle with the chicken strips, then drizzle with the chutney and extra yoghurt. Cook in the oven for 15–20 minutes, or until the base is crisp and golden.

4 Sprinkle with the fresh coriander leaves and garnish with some snow pea sprouts. Cut into slices and serve immediately.

nutrition per serve
Fat 32 g; Protein 97.5 g; Carbohydrate 118 g; Dietary Fibre 11 g; Cholesterol 240 mg; 4855 kJ (1160 Cal)

variation

You can use Turkish bread as a pizza base. Cut into four 12 cm (4 1/2 inch) square pieces, then split through the middle so that you have eight squares.

ingredients

- 1 kg (2 lb) chicken mince
- 1 cup (80 g/2¾ oz) fresh white breadcrumbs (2 slices day-old bread)
- ¼ cup (60 ml/2 fl oz) puréed tomatoes
- 1 onion, grated
- 2 eggs, lightly beaten
- 2 tablespoons finely chopped fresh flat-leaf parsley
- 2 tablespoons Worcestershire sauce
- ⅓ cup (80 ml/2¾ fl oz) barbecue sauce

preparation: 15 minutes
cooking: 1 hour 15 minutes
serves: 4–6

1 Preheat the oven to moderate 180°C (350°F/Gas 4). Lightly grease a 1.5 litre (20 x 11 cm/8 x 4½ inch) loaf tin. Put the chicken mince, breadcrumbs, tomato, onion, egg, parsley, Worcestershire sauce, 2 tablespoons of the barbecue sauce and a little salt and freshly ground black pepper in a bowl and mix together thoroughly.

2 Press the chicken mixture into the prepared loaf tin. Place the tin on an oven tray to catch any juices that may spill over the side, and bake for 1 hour.

3 Pour off any excess fat from the tin. Spread the remaining barbecue sauce over the top of the meatloaf and bake for a further 15 minutes. Turn out the meatloaf and serve sliced with a salad and extra barbecue sauce, if desired.

nutrition per serve (6)
Fat 6 g; Protein 40 g; Carbohydrate 15 g; Dietary Fibre 1 g; Cholesterol 145 mg; 1175 kJ (280 cal)

variation

You can add any fresh herbs you have on hand to this meatloaf, such as basil, coriander, chives or thyme. If you have any left over, it is delicious served cold.

sichuan chicken

ingredients

- ¼ teaspoon five-spice powder
- 750 g (1½ lb) chicken thigh fillets, halved
- 2 tablespoons peanut oil
- 1 tablespoon julienned fresh ginger
- 1 teaspoon Sichuan peppercorns, crushed
- 1 teaspoon chilli bean paste
- 2 tablespoons soy sauce
- 1 tablespoon Chinese rice wine
- 1¼ cups (250 g/8 oz) jasmine rice
- 600 g (1¼ lb) baby bok choy, leaves separated

preparation: 10 minutes
cooking: 25 minutes
serves: 4

1 Sprinkle the five-spice powder over the chicken. Heat a wok until very hot, add half the oil and swirl to coat the side of the wok. Add the chicken and cook for 2 minutes on each side, or until browned. Remove from the wok.

2 Reduce the heat to medium and cook the ginger for 30 seconds. Add the peppercorns and chilli bean paste. Return the chicken to the wok, add the soy sauce, wine and ½ cup (125 ml/4 fl oz) water, then simmer for 15–20 minutes, or until the chicken is cooked through.

3 Meanwhile, bring a large saucepan of water to the boil. Add the rice and cook for 12 minutes, stirring occasionally. Drain well.

4 Heat the remaining oil in a saucepan. Add the bok choy and toss gently for 1 minute, or until the leaves wilt and the stems are tender. Serve with the chicken and steamed rice.

nutrition per serve
Fat 23.5 g; Protein 42 g; Carbohydrate 52 g; Dietary Fibre 2.5 g; Cholesterol 163 mg; 2465 kJ (590 Cal)

shopping tip

Chilli bean paste is red or brown in colour and is sometimes called hot bean paste. It is available at most large supermarkets. Some brands of paste are very hot, so use with caution.
You can replace the chilli bean paste with ½–1 teaspoon chilli flakes or sambal oelek.

ingredients

800 g (1 lb 10 oz) chicken breast or thigh fillets, trimmed
1 egg, lightly beaten
cornflour, to coat
oil for deep-frying
1/2 cup (125 ml/4 fl oz) lemon juice
1 tablespoon white vinegar
1/4 cup (60 g/2 oz) sugar
1 1/2 tablespoons cornflour
2 spring onions, sliced on the diagonal
lemon wedges, to serve

preparation: 15 minutes
cooking: 20 minutes
serves: 4

1 Season the chicken with salt and freshly ground black pepper. Coat with the egg, then the cornflour, shaking off any excess.

2 Fill a wok or heavy-based saucepan one-third full of oil and heat to 180°C (350°F), or until a cube of bread dropped into the oil browns in 15 seconds. Add the chicken in batches and cook for 6 minutes, or until golden brown and cooked through. Drain on crumpled paper towels.

3 Combine the lemon juice, vinegar, sugar and 1/4 cup (60 ml/2 fl oz) water in a small saucepan, and stir over low heat until the sugar dissolves. Bring to the boil, then reduce the heat and simmer for 1–2 minutes. Combine the cornflour with 1/4 cup (60 ml/2 fl oz) water, add to the pan and mix well. Cook for 1 minute, or until the sauce boils and thickens.

4 To serve, slice the chicken, spoon on the sauce and garnish with the spring onion and lemon. Serve with rice.

nutrition per serve
Fat 15 g; Protein 47 g; Carbohydrate 20 g; Dietary Fibre 0 g; Cholesterol 145 mg; 1740 kJ (416 Cal)

cooking hint

To ensure that you get an evenly crisp coating on the chicken make sure that the oil is very hot and that you do not overcrowd the wok during cooking.

beef & veal

beef stroganoff

ingredients

600 g (1 1/4 lb) rib eye fillet or rump
1/4 cup (30 g/1 oz) seasoned plain flour
375 g (12 oz) fettucine
60 g (2 oz) butter
1 small onion, finely chopped
300 g (10 oz) button mushrooms, thickly sliced
1 tablespoon tomato paste
1/4 cup (60 ml/2 fl oz) red wine
300 ml (9 1/2 fl oz) cream

preparation: 10 minutes
cooking: 20 minutes
serves: 4

1 Place the slices of beef between two sheets of plastic wrap and pound with a rolling pin until half their thickness. Cut each slice into strips about 1 cm (1/2 inch) wide. Place in a plastic bag with the seasoned flour and shake to coat.
2 Bring a large saucepan of water to the boil and cook the pasta according to the packet instructions, until *al dente*.
3 Meanwhile, melt 40 g (1 1/4 oz) of the butter in a frying pan over medium heat and cook the onion for 2 minutes. Add the beef in batches and cook for 5 minutes, or until evenly browned. Remove from the pan and keep warm. Heat the remaining butter in the pan and add the mushrooms, stirring, for 2–3 minutes, or until soft and lightly browned. Add the tomato paste and the red wine, stirring continuously for 2 minutes, or until the sauce has reduced. Add the beef, stir in the cream, then reduce the heat to medium–low and simmer gently for a further minute, or until the sauce has thickened. Serve with the pasta.

nutrition per serve
Fat 53.5 g; Protein 47 g; Carbohydrate 73.5 g; Dietary Fibre 5.5 g; Cholesterol 243 mg; 4085 kJ (975 Cal)

variation

You can use any long pasta—try tagliatelle or pappardelle. The long strands get a lovely coating of the sauce.

ingredients

- 2 cloves garlic, crushed
- 1/4 cup (60 ml/2 fl oz) kecap manis
- 2 1/2 teaspoons sambal oelek
- 1/2 teaspoon ground coriander
- 1 tablespoon grated palm sugar or soft brown sugar
- 1 teaspoon sesame oil
- 400 g (13 oz) beef fillet, partially frozen, thinly sliced
- 1 tablespoon peanut oil
- 2 tablespoons chopped toasted peanuts
- 3 tablespoons chopped fresh coriander leaves

preparation: 5 minutes + 20 minutes marinating
cooking: 10 minutes
serves: 4

1 Combine the garlic, kecap manis, sambal oelek, ground coriander, grated palm sugar, sesame oil and 2 tablespoons water in a large bowl and mix. Add the beef and coat well. Cover with plastic wrap and refrigerate for 20 minutes.

2 Heat a wok over high heat, add the peanut oil and swirl to coat. Add the meat in batches and cook each batch for 2–3 minutes, or until nicely browned.

3 Arrange the beef on a serving platter, sprinkle with the chopped peanuts and fresh coriander, and serve with steamed rice.

nutrition per serve
Fat 13.5 g; Protein 24 g; Carbohydrate 5.5 g; Dietary Fibre 1 g; Cholesterol 67 mg; 985 kJ (235 Cal)

cooking hint

Partially freezing the beef makes it far easier to slice thinly. If it is already fully frozen, allow the beef to thaw just a little before slicing. However, don't freeze meat that has been frozen and thawed.
If kecap manis is unavailable, use soy sauce sweetened with a little soft brown sugar.

serves: 4

60 simple steak sauces

PAN-FRIED STEAKS

Trim four 2.5 cm (1 inch) thick sirloin or fillet steaks of excess sinew and fat. Season both sides of the steaks lightly with freshly ground black pepper and salt. Heat 20 g (3/4 oz) butter and 1 tablespoon olive oil in a frying pan over medium heat until the butter melts. Increase the heat to medium–high and cook for 1 1/2–2 minutes on each side for rare, 3 minutes on each side for medium or 4 minutes on each side for well done. Remove from the pan, cover and keep warm while you make your sauce.

serves 4

creamy dijon sauce

Add 20 g (3/4 oz) butter to the same pan, melt over low heat, then add 2 finely chopped French shallots and cook over medium–high heat for 1–2 minutes, or until softened. Add 150 ml (5 fl oz) dry white wine, stir to loosen any sediment on the bottom of the pan and cook for 1 minute. Add 1 1/2 cups (375 ml/ 12 fl oz) beef stock, increase the heat to high, bring to the boil and cook for 5 minutes, or until reduced by half. Whisk in 1/4 cup (60 g/2 oz) Dijon mustard until combined. Stir in 1/3 cup (80 ml/ 2 3/4 fl oz) thick cream and simmer, stirring occasionally, for 5 minutes, or until thickened. Season and serve over the steaks.

diane sauce

Add 20 g (3/4 oz) butter to the same frying pan and melt over low heat. Add 4 finely chopped spring onions and 4 cloves finely chopped garlic and cook, stirring, over medium heat for about 1 minute. Pour in 2 tablespoons Worcestershire sauce and 1 tablespoon brandy and stir to loosen any sediment on the bottom of the pan. Stir in 1/2 cup (125 ml/ 4 fl oz) cream, reduce the heat and simmer for 4–5 minutes, or until reduced and thickened. Season with salt and pepper and serve spooned over the steaks.

quick onion gravy

Add 20 g (¾ oz) butter and 1 tablespoon olive oil to the same pan. Heat over low heat and, when the butter has melted, cook 2 thinly sliced onions and 1 teaspoon chopped fresh thyme over high heat for 4–5 minutes, or until the onion is lightly browned and softened. Deglaze the pan with ⅓ cup (80 ml/2¾ fl oz) dry white wine and boil until nearly all the liquid has evaporated. Sprinkle with 2 teaspoons plain flour and cook for a further 2 minutes, then add ¾ cup (185 ml/6 fl oz) beef stock. Simmer for 1 minute, or until thickened. Season to taste and serve over the steaks.

pizzaiola sauce

Add an extra tablespoon of olive oil to the pan and heat over low heat. Cook 3 cloves crushed garlic for 1 minute, or until just beginning to brown. Add a 400 g (13 oz) can Italian chopped tomatoes and 2 teaspoons dried oregano, increase the heat to high and simmer for 5 minutes. Add ¼ cup (80 g/2¾ oz) pitted and halved Kalamata olives and salt and pepper to taste, and simmer for a further 1–2 minutes. Pour the sauce over the steaks and sprinkle with chopped fresh flat-leaf parsley.

cooking hint

When cooking steaks, a quick test for doneness is to press the steak with your index finger as it cooks. If the steak feels soft and flexible, it is rare; if it gives a little, it is medium; and if it feels firm and does not spring back at all, then it is well done.

If your prefer your steak piping hot, return it to the pan with the sauce for about 1 minute before serving.

From left to right: Creamy Dijon sauce, Diane sauce, Quick onion gravy, Pizzaiola sauce.

chilli con carne soup

ingredients

- 1.25 litres beef stock
- 1 tablespoon olive oil
- 1 onion, finely chopped
- 300 g (10 oz) lean beef mince
- 1 clove garlic, crushed
- 3 teaspoons paprika
- 2 teaspoons cumin seeds
- 2 tablespoons tomato paste
- 440 g (14 oz) can red kidney beans, rinsed and drained
- 1/3 cup (80 g/2 3/4 oz) sour cream

preparation: 10 minutes
cooking: 25 minutes
serves: 4

1 Pour the stock into a saucepan and bring slowly to the boil over medium heat.

2 Heat the oil in a large heavy-based saucepan. Add the onion and cook, stirring, for 5 minutes, or until softened. Add the beef mince and cook until browned, breaking up any lumps with a fork. Stir in the garlic, paprika and cumin seeds and cook for a further 1 minute.

3 Pour the stock into the saucepan with the mince, then stir in the tomato paste and mix together well. Bring to the boil, then reduce the heat to low, add the drained kidney beans and simmer for 15 minutes, or until the soup has slightly thickened.

4 Divide the soup evenly among four warm soup bowls and top with a dollop of the sour cream. Season to taste with salt and freshly ground black pepper.

nutrition per serve
Fat 20 g; Protein 30 g; Carbohydrate 20 g; Dietary Fibre 13 g; Cholesterol 65 mg; 1550 kJ (370 Cal)

serving tip

Soft flour tortillas make an ideal companion to this soup. Warm them on both sides in a dry, non-stick frying pan over medium heat for 1–2 minutes, then cut into quarters.
Paprika varies in taste from mildly hot (Hungarian) to mildly sweet.

veal goulash with caraway noodles

ingredients

- 1/4 cup (60 ml/2 fl oz) oil
- 1 kg (2 lb) veal shoulder, diced
- 1 large onion, thinly sliced
- 3 cloves garlic, finely chopped
- 1/4 cup (60 g/2 oz) paprika
- 1/2 teaspoon caraway seeds
- 2 x 400 g (13 oz) cans chopped tomatoes, one can drained
- 350 g (11 oz) fresh fettucine
- 40 g (1 1/4 oz) butter, softened

preparation: 10 minutes
cooking: 1 hour 35 minutes
serves: 4

1 Heat half the oil in a large saucepan over medium–high heat, then brown the meat in batches for 3 minutes. Remove the veal from the pan and set aside with any pan juices.

2 Add the remaining oil to the pan and sauté the onion and garlic over medium heat for 5 minutes, or until softened. Add the paprika and 1/4 teaspoon of the caraway seeds and stir for 30 seconds.

3 Add the chopped tomatoes and 1/2 cup (125 ml/4 fl oz) water. Return the veal to the pan with any juices, increase the heat to high and bring to the boil. Cover with a lid, reduce the heat to low, then allow to simmer for 1 1/4 hours, or until the meat is tender and the sauce has thickened.

4 About 15 minutes before the veal is ready, cook the pasta in a large saucepan of rapidly boiling salted water, according to the packet instructions, until *al dente*. Drain, then return to the pan. Stir in the butter and the remaining caraway seeds. Serve immediately with the goulash.

nutrition per serve
Fat 25 g; Protein 67.5 g; Carbohydrate 72.5 g; Dietary Fibre 10 g; Cholesterol 230 mg; 3340 kJ (800 Cal)

cooking hint

Make sure the saucepan is very hot before adding the meat or it will stew rather than brown in the pan and the result will be chewy, tough meat.

64 pan-fried veal cutlets with celeriac and potato mash

ingredients

- 2 teaspoons olive oil
- 100 g (3½ oz) butter
- 4 large veal cutlets, about 2 cm (¾ inch) thick
- ½ cup (10 g/¼ oz) fresh sage
- 500 g (1 lb) floury potatoes (e.g. King Edward, russet or Pontiac), cut into cubes
- 750 g (1½ lb) celeriac, peeled and cut into cubes
- ¼ cup (60 ml/2 fl oz) lemon juice
- 2 tablespoons cream

preparation: 10 minutes
cooking: 35 minutes
serves: 4

1 Preheat the oven to moderate 180°C (350°F/Gas 4). Heat the oil and 25 g (¾ oz) of the butter in a large frying pan over medium heat. Add the cutlets and cook for 1–2 minutes on each side, or until browned. Transfer to a roasting tin. Add the sage to the frying pan, toss through the cooking juices, then place the leaves on top of the cutlets. Bake for 12–15 minutes, or until the meat is slightly springy to the touch.

2 While the cutlets are cooking, bring 2 saucepans of salted water to the boil and cook the potato and celeriac separately for 8–10 minutes, or until tender. Drain. Return the potato to the pan, add the cream and 50 g (1¾ oz) of the butter and mash smooth. Purée the celeriac in a food processor, then add to the potato. Stir well; season to taste.

3 When the cutlets are cooked, remove from the oven and cover loosely with foil to keep warm. Add the lemon juice and remaining butter to the frying pan and cook over low heat, scraping up any sediment with a wooden spoon. Add any juices from the roasting tin, season to taste and gently warm through. Transfer the cutlets to serving plates, spoon on the sauce and serve with the mash.

nutrition per serve
Fat 35 g; Protein 85 g; Carbohydrate 27 g; Dietary Fibre 10 g; Cholesterol 370 mg; 3255 kJ (778 Cal)

variation

This recipe can also be made using pork or lamb chops; the cooking times will vary according to the thickness of the meat.

beef with red wine sauce and bean purée

ingredients

- 1/3 cup (80 ml/2 3/4 fl oz) virgin olive oil
- 3 large cloves garlic, crushed
- 800 g (1 lb 10 oz) beef eye fillet
- 2 x 310 g (10 oz) cans cannellini beans
- 3 cups (750 ml/24 fl oz) beef stock
- 1 1/3 cups (350 ml/11 fl oz) red wine
- 1/3 cup (90 g/3 oz) tomato paste
- 2 tablespoons soft brown sugar

preparation: 15 minutes + 30 minutes marinating + 15 minutes resting
cooking: 40 minutes
serves: 4

1 Place the oil and 1 crushed garlic clove in a bowl, and mix well. Add the beef and toss well. Marinate for 30 minutes. Preheat the oven to moderately hot 200°C (400°F/Gas 6).

2 Rinse and drain the beans, then place in a food processor or blender with the remaining garlic and blend smooth. With the motor running, gradually add 1/4 cup (60 ml/2 fl oz) of the beef stock and process until smooth. Season.

3 Heat a large, deep frying pan over medium heat, add the beef and, brushing with the marinade, cook for 5 minutes, or until browned all over. Place in a roasting tin and roast for 15–20 minutes, or until cooked to your liking. Cover and rest for 15 minutes.

4 Meanwhile, add the wine to the pan and stir, scraping the bottom to remove any sediment. Add the remaining stock, tomato paste and sugar to the pan, then reduce the heat and simmer for 25–30 minutes, or until the sauce has reduced by half. Place the bean purée in a small saucepan and gently heat. To serve, slice the beef. Divide the bean purée among four plates and arrange the beef over the top. Spoon on the wine sauce, season with pepper and garnish with thyme sprigs, if desired. Serve with steamed greens.

nutrition per serve
Fat 30 g; Protein 54 g; Carbohydrate 30 g; Dietary Fibre 11 g; Cholesterol 134 mg; 2685 kJ (640 Cal)

storage hint

Any leftover bean purée can be eaten cold the next day as a dip with fresh Turkish bread or as part of an antipasto plate.

72 veal schnitzel crumb mixtures

VEAL SCHNITZEL

Flatten four 125 g (4 oz) veal steaks between two pieces of plastic wrap by beating gently with a meat mallet until they are 5 mm (¼ inch) thick. Lightly season each steak on both sides with salt and freshly ground black pepper.

Place ⅓ cup (40 g/1¼ oz) well-seasoned plain flour in one shallow bowl, 2 lightly beaten eggs in a second and your breadcrumb coating in a third. If you are making plain schnitzel, use 2 cups (160 g/5½ oz) fresh or 1 cup (100 g/3½ oz) dry breadcrumbs. Dip each veal steak in the flour and shake off the excess. Next, dip the veal into the egg, then coat in the breadcrumbs.

Heat ½ cup (125 ml/4 fl oz) olive oil in a large frying pan and cook the veal in two batches over medium–high heat for 2–3 minutes on each side, or until golden and cooked through. Drain on paper towels, then serve immediately with lemon wedges.

serves 4

gremolata crumbs

Place 2 cups (160 g/5½ oz) fresh or 1 cup (100 g/3½ oz) dry breadcrumbs, 3 tablespoons finely chopped fresh flat-leaf parsley, 2 cloves crushed garlic and 3 teaspoons finely grated lemon rind in a bowl and mix together.

parmesan crumbs

Mix together 1 cup (80 g/2¾ oz) fresh or ½ cup (50 g/1¾ oz) dry breadcrumbs with 1 cup (100 g/ 3½ oz) grated Parmesan and 2 tablespoons finely chopped fresh flat-leaf parsley.

almond and thyme crumbs

Place 2 cups (160 g/5½ oz) fresh or 1 cup (100 g/3½ oz) dry breadcrumbs, ½ cup (55 g/2 oz) coarsely ground blanched almonds and 3 teaspoons chopped fresh thyme in a bowl and mix well.

ham and cheese pockets

Lay a steak flat on a work surface. Cut a thin slice of Cheddar or Gruyère cheese and a slice of leg ham to half the size of the steak. Lay the cheese and ham on one end of the steak. Brush all around the edge of the steak with beaten egg, then fold the steak in half so that it is enclosing the ham and cheese. Trim the edges to make sure no filling is protruding from the edges. Pound the edges of the steaks together to seal. Repeat with the other three steaks. Crumb and cook as normal.

cooking hint

Make sure the oil is very hot before you put the schnitzels in the pan or they will soak up too much oil and become soggy. Don't be tempted to keep moving the schnitzels around the frying pan while cooking or the crust will stick to the pan.

From left to right: Gremolata schnitzel, Parmesan schnitzel, Almond and thyme schnitzel, Ham and cheese pockets.

veal shanks with cheesy potatoes, tomato and pancetta

ingredients

- 12 sun-dried tomatoes in oil, drained
- 6 slices mild pancetta, cut into strips
- 4 veal shanks (450 g/14 oz each), trimmed, knuckle removed
- 1 large sprig fresh rosemary, leaves removed and chopped
- 1 cup (250 ml/8 fl oz) red wine
- 900 g (1 lb 13 oz) waxy potatoes, cut into chunks
- 250 g (8 oz) mascarpone
- 1 cup (100 g/3½ oz) grated Parmesan

preparation: 15 minutes
cooking: 1 hour 45 minutes
serves: 4

1 Preheat the oven to moderate 180°C (350°F/Gas 4). Drain the tomatoes, reserving the oil. Heat 1 tablespoon of the oil in a frying pan, add the pancetta and cook over high heat for 3–4 minutes, or until browned and crisp. Remove the pancetta from the pan. Add the shanks two at a time and cook, turning, for 3–4 minutes, or until browned on all sides.

2 Thinly slice the tomatoes, place in a bowl with the rosemary and pancetta, and mix together well. Place the shanks in a casserole dish with the red wine, half the tomato mixture, ½ cup (125 ml/4 fl oz) water, and salt and black pepper. Cook, covered, in the oven for 1½ hours, or until cooked.

3 Meanwhile, bring a saucepan of lightly salted water to the boil, add the potato and cook for 10–15 minutes, or until soft. Drain, return to the saucepan and mash. Stir in the mascarpone and half the Parmesan. Keep warm. Add the remaining Parmesan to the remaining tomato mixture. To serve, put a generous serve of mashed potato on each plate, top with a shank and some of the sauce. Sprinkle the tomato mixture over the top and serve

nutrition per serve
Fat 36 g; Protein 45 g; Carbohydrate 32 g; Dietary Fibre 4 g; Cholesterol 152 mg; 2808 kJ (670 Cal)

cooking hint

If you prefer a softer mash, add 2–3 tablespoons of hot milk. If pancetta is unavailable you can use 6 rashers bacon instead.

beef medallions with french shallots and creamy spinach

ingredients

- 16 French shallots, peeled
- 2 tablespoons light olive oil
- 1.25 kg ($2\frac{1}{2}$ lb) beef eye fillet, trimmed
- 1 cup (250 ml/8 fl oz) red wine
- 2 tablespoons soft brown sugar
- 2 tablespoons balsamic vinegar
- 1 kg (2 lb) English spinach
- $\frac{1}{4}$ cup (60 ml/2 fl oz) thick cream

preparation: 15 minutes
cooking: 40 minutes
serves: 4

1 Preheat the oven to moderately hot 200°C (400°F/Gas 6). Bring a saucepan of lightly salted water to the boil, add the shallots and cook for 1 minute. Drain reserving 1 cup (250 ml/8 fl oz) of the water. Heat 1 tablespoon oil in a frying pan, add the eye fillet and brown on all sides. Place the fillet in a roasting tin and roast for 20 minutes, or until cooked to your liking. Cover and keep warm. Meanwhile, put the wine and $\frac{3}{4}$ cup (185 ml/6 fl oz) shallot water in the frying pan and bring to the boil. Boil for 5 minutes, or until reduced to 1 cup (250 ml/8 fl oz). Season.

2 Heat the remaining oil in a clean frying pan, add the shallots and cook, stirring, over medium heat for 10 minutes, or until browned all over. Add the sugar and cook for 2 minutes, or until melted, then add the vinegar and cook for 10 minutes, or until caramelised.

3 Place the spinach and remaining shallot water in a saucepan over medium heat and cook for 2–3 minutes, or until the spinach has wilted. Add the cream and season with salt and pepper. Reheat the red wine sauce. Slice the beef into neat medallions. Place a portion of creamed spinach on each plate and top with a beef medallion and four caramelised shallots. Drizzle with a little red wine sauce and season with pepper.

nutrition per serve
Fat 33 g; Protein 88 g; Carbohydrate 11 g; Dietary Fibre 1.5 g; Cholesterol 272 mg; 3061 kJ (730 cal)

shopping tip

French shallots are members of the onion family that grow in small clusters and have a sweet flavour. When selecting French shallots, look for ones that are similar in size so that they will cook evenly.

lamb

86 lamb shanks in rich tomato sauce

ingredients

- 2 tablespoons olive oil
- 1 large red onion, thinly sliced
- 4 x 250 g (8 oz) French-trimmed lamb shanks
- 2 cloves garlic, crushed
- 400 g (13 oz) can peeled chopped tomatoes
- 1/2 cup (125 ml/4 fl oz) red wine
- 2 teaspoons finely chopped fresh rosemary
- 1 cup (150 g/5 oz) instant polenta
- 50 g (1 3/4 oz) butter
- 1/2 cup (50 g/1 3/4 oz) grated Parmesan

preparation: 10 minutes
cooking: 2 hours 30 minutes
serves: 4

1 Preheat the oven to warm 160°C (315°F/Gas 2–3). Heat the oil in a 4 litre flameproof casserole dish over medium heat and sauté the onion for 3–4 minutes, or until just softening. Add the lamb and cook for 2–3 minutes, or until browned. Add the garlic, tomato and wine, then bring to the boil and cook for 3 minutes. Stir in the rosemary and 1/4 teaspoon each of salt and pepper.
2 Cover, transfer to the oven and cook for 2 hours. Remove the lid and cook for a further 15 minutes, or until the lamb is just starting to fall off the bone. Check periodically that the sauce is not too dry, adding water if necessary.
3 About 20 minutes before serving, bring 1 litre water to the boil in a large saucepan. Add the polenta in a thin stream, beating continuously with a whisk to incorporate into the water. Reduce the heat to very low and simmer for 8–10 minutes, or until thick and coming away from the sides of the pan. Stir in the butter and Parmesan and season.
4 To serve, spoon the polenta onto four serving plates and place the shanks on top. Spoon a little sauce from the casserole on the shanks.

nutrition per serve
Fat 36.5 g; Protein 39 g; Carbohydrate 31 g; Dietary Fibre 3 g; Cholesterol 137 mg; 2615 kJ (625 Cal)

shopping tip

French-trimmed lamb shanks are shanks that have been trimmed back to the bone by about 4 cm (1 1/2 inch). You can do it yourself, but you can save a lot of time by asking your butcher to do it for you.

lamb fillets with spicy lentils

ingredients

- 1/2 cup (125 g/4 oz) plain yoghurt
- 2 tablespoons finely chopped fresh mint
- 1/2 teaspoon chilli powder
- 1 tablespoon garam masala, dry-roasted
- 3 teaspoons ground cumin, dry-roasted
- 1/3 cup (80 ml/2 3/4 fl oz) oil
- 4 x 150 g (5 oz) lamb backstraps
- 2 teaspoons grated fresh ginger
- 1 teaspoon ground turmeric
- 2 x 425 g (14 oz) cans lentils, drained and rinsed

preparation: 15 minutes + 10 minutes marinating
cooking: 20 minutes
serves: 4

1 Combine the yoghurt and half the mint in a small non-metallic bowl. Cover and set aside.

2 Place the garam masala in a small dry frying pan over medium heat for 1 minute, or until fragrant. Remove from the pan, then repeat with the cumin. Combine the chilli, 2 teaspoons of the garam masala, 2 teaspoons of the cumin and 2 tablespoons of the oil. Place the lamb in a non-metallic dish and brush with the spiced oil. Cover and marinate for at least 10 minutes, or overnight, if time permits.

3 Meanwhile, heat 1 tablespoon of the oil in a saucepan. Add the ginger, turmeric and remaining cumin and cook for 30 seconds, or until fragrant. Add the lentils, stir thoroughly, then bring to a simmer. Reduce the heat to low, add the remaining garam masala and season well with salt. Cook, covered, for 5 minutes, adding 1/4 cup (60 ml/2 fl oz) water if the lentils start to stick. Before serving, stir in the remaining mint.

4 Heat a large frying pan over medium–high heat and add the remaining oil. Add the backstraps and sear on all sides, then turn and cook for 3–4 minutes on each side for medium rare, or until cooked to your liking. Allow to rest for several minutes, then cut into 1 cm (1/2 inch) slices on the diagonal.

5 To serve, place a small mound of lentils on a plate, arrange the lamb slices on top and serve with a dollop of mint raita. Garnish with fresh mint, if desired.

nutrition per serve
Fat 24.5 g; Protein 40 g; Carbohydrate 15 g; Dietary Fibre 5 g; Cholesterol 102 mg; 1840 kJ (440 Cal)

cooking hint

Allowing the meat to rest makes the meat more tender and juicy.

shepherd's pie with garlic mash

ingredients

- 1½ tablespoons oil
- 1 large onion, diced
- 1 carrot, finely diced
- 8 cloves garlic, peeled
- 750 g (1½ lb) lean lamb mince
- 1½ cups (375 ml/12 fl oz) Italian tomato passata
- 300 ml (9½ fl oz) beef stock
- 800 g (1 lb 10 oz) potatoes, cut into large chunks
- 30 g (1 oz) butter

preparation: 15 minutes
cooking: 1 hour 40 minutes
serves: 4

1 Heat the oil in a saucepan over medium heat. Add the onion and carrot, and cook for 5 minutes, or until soft. Crush 2 garlic cloves and sauté with the onion for another minute. Add the lamb mince and stir well, breaking up any lumps with the back of a wooden spoon. Cook for 5 minutes, or until browned and cooked through. Drain off any excess fat with a large spoon, then add the tomato passata and 1 cup (250 ml/8 fl oz) of the stock. Cover and bring to the boil. Reduce the heat to medium–low and simmer for 25 minutes. Uncover and cook for a further 20 minutes, or until the sauce reduces and thickens. Preheat the oven to moderately hot 200°C (400°F/Gas 6).

2 Meanwhile, place the potato in a saucepan of boiling water with the remaining garlic and cook for 15–20 minutes, or until tender. Drain well, then return to the saucepan over low heat, stirring to evaporate any excess water. Remove from the heat, add the butter and the remaining stock and mash with a potato masher until smooth. Season.

3 Transfer the lamb to a [illegible].5 litre ovenproof ceramic dish. Spoon the mashed potato over the meat mixture and spread it out evenly. Use a fork to swirl the surface. Bake for 40 minutes, or until the potato is golden brown. Season to taste and serve immediately.

nutrition per serve
Fat 27 g; Protein 48.5 g; Carbohydrate 42 g; Dietary Fibre 9.5 g; Cholesterol 149 mg; 2545 kJ (610 Cal)

storage hint

Shepherd's pie is a great meal to store in the freezer ready to be pulled out when needed. It will last for up to 3 months.

ingredients

1 red capsicum
1 yellow capsicum
1 green capsicum
300 g (10 oz) lean lamb mince
2 teaspoons chopped fresh thyme
2 tablespoons chopped fresh parsley
2 tomatoes, seeded and finely chopped
1 large onion, finely chopped
1/3 cup (25 g/3/4 oz) fresh breadcrumbs
1 egg white, lightly beaten
4 slices cheese
1 red onion, thinly sliced
2 teaspoons olive oil
4 hamburger buns
40 g (1 1/4 oz) rocket

preparation: 30 minutes
cooking: 1 hour
serves: 4

1 Cut the capsicums into quarters and remove the membranes and seeds. Grill skin-side up, until the skin blackens and blisters. Place in a bowl and cover with plastic wrap. When cool enough to handle, peel off the skin and cut the capsicums into strips.
2 Place the mince, thyme, parsley, tomato, onion, breadcrumbs, egg white and 1 teaspoon ground black pepper in a bowl and mix together. Form into four even-sized patties. Heat a non-stick frying pan over medium heat and cook the patties on each side for 5 minutes, or until cooked. Put a slice of cheese on top to melt slightly. Remove from the pan. Cook the onion in the olive oil for 4–5 minutes over medium heat until softened a little. Cut the buns in half and toast each side until crisp.
3 To assemble, layer the bun with a little rocket, the patty with cheese, onion, one strip each of red, yellow and green capsicum, and top with more rocket and the top of the bun. Cut in half and serve with wedges, if desired.

nutrition per serve
Fat 17 g; Protein 30 g; Carbohydrate 39.5 g; Dietary Fibre 2.5 g; Cholesterol 72.5 mg; 1815 kJ (435 Cal)

serving tip

The burgers are great with potato wedges. To make wedges, preheat the oven to moderately hot (200°C (400°F/Gas 6). Cut 400 g (13 oz) Pontiac or desiree potatoes into wedges. Toss in 1 tablespoon olive oil, season well and bake in a single layer for 40 minutes, or until crisp and golden, turning once during cooking.

orange and oregano lamb with tomato bocconcini salad

ingredients

- 1 kg (2 lb) lamb fillets, trimmed
- 1/4 cup (60 ml/2 fl oz) orange juice
- 2 cloves garlic, crushed
- 1/4 cup (60 ml/2 fl oz) balsamic vinegar
- 2 tablespoons fresh oregano leaves
- 1/4 cup (60 ml/2 fl oz) extra virgin olive oil
- 6 ripe Roma tomatoes, cut into thick slices
- 200 g (6 1/2 oz) bocconcini, cut into 5 mm (1/4 inch) thick slices

preparation: 15 minutes + 1 hour marinating + 5 minutes resting
cooking: 10 minutes
serves: 4

1 Place the lamb in a non-metallic dish with the combined orange juice, garlic, 2 tablespoons of the balsamic vinegar and 1 tablespoon finely chopped oregano leaves. Cover and leave to marinate for 1 hour in the refrigerator. Drain, reserving the marinade.

2 Heat a chargrill pan to hot and brush with 2 tablespoons of the oil. Add the lamb and cook over high heat for 3–5 minutes on each side, or until cooked to your liking. Rest for 5 minutes. Meanwhile, place the marinade in a saucepan, bring to the boil, then reduce the heat and simmer for 2 minutes. Cut the lamb on the diagonal into 2 cm (3/4 inch) thick slices.

3 Arrange the tomato on four serving plates and place a slice of bocconcini over each piece of tomato. Place the remaining olive oil and balsamic vinegar in a bowl, mix together well, then drizzle over the bocconcini. Arrange the lamb over the top. Drizzle with the marinade and garnish with the remaining oregano.

nutrition per serve
Fat 40 g; Protein 70 g; Carbohydrate 4.5 g; Dietary Fibre 2 g; Cholesterol 216 mg; 2755 kJ (660 Cal)

storage hint

Bocconcini are small balls of fresh mozzarella cheese usually made out of cow's milk. They are available from delicatessens and some large supermarkets. Keep the cheese refrigerated and covered in the whey in which it is sold The bocconcini will last for up to 3 weeks but should be discarded if it shows any signs of yellowing.

fennel lamb with roasted garlic and parsnip mash

ingredients

- 1 heaped tablespoon fennel seeds
- 2 tablespoons olive oil
- 2 x 6 racks of lamb, trimmed
- 6 large cloves garlic, unpeeled
- 4 large parsnips, peeled and chopped
- 1/3 cup (80 ml/2 3/4 fl oz) cream
- 2 tablespoons golden syrup

preparation: 15 minutes
cooking: 30 minutes
serves: 4

1 Preheat the oven to moderately hot 200°C (400°F/Gas 6). Place a roasting tin, with a wire rack in it, into the oven to heat. Lightly crush the fennel seeds, then place in a large bowl. Mix in the olive oil and some salt and freshly ground black pepper. Toss the lamb racks in the mixture, then drain, reserving 1 tablespoon of the oil.

2 Heat the reserved oil in a large frying pan and cook the racks of lamb for 2–3 minutes on each side, or until browned. Transfer to the hot roasting tin and roast for 20–25 minutes, or until tender. Add the whole garlic cloves in the last 10 minutes and roast until soft. Cool slightly, then peel.

3 Meanwhile, bring a large saucepan of lightly salted water to the boil. Add the parsnip and cook for 8–10 minutes, or until tender. Drain, then place in a food processor with the roasted garlic, cream and 1 tablespoon golden syrup. Process until smooth, and season with salt and pepper. Slice the lamb and arrange three cutlets on each plate. Serve with the creamy parsnip mash, drizzled with the remaining golden syrup. Delicious with steamed vegetables.

nutrition per serve
Fat 27 g; Protein 58 g; Carbohydrate 24 g; Dietary Fibre 4 g; Cholesterol 192 mg; 2402 kJ (579 Cal)

variation

The fennel seed can be replaced by a blend of lightly crushed cumin and coriander seeds.
Trimming the lamb racks removes excess fat and sinew from the bones which would otherwise burn during cooking. It is usually done by the butcher and is mainly for aesthetic purposes.

spicy coatings for lamb cutlets

CHARGRILLED LAMB CUTLETS

Make your spice rub from the adjacent recipes. Brush eight lamb cutlets with oil, then coat them with a generous amount of your spice rub and set aside for about 30 minutes. Preheat a lightly greased chargrill pan over medium heat and grill the chops for 4 minutes on each side, or until cooked to your liking.

serves 4

cajun rub

Place 2 tablespoons dried onion powder, 1 tablespoon dried basil, 1 tablespoon paprika, 1 tablespoon garlic powder, 2 teaspoons cayenne pepper and ½ teaspoon each of dried oregano, dried parsley, dried thyme, salt and ground white pepper in a small bowl and mix.

cumin and coriander rub

Dry-fry 2 tablespoons coriander seeds, 1 tablespoon fennel seeds and 1 tablespoon cumin seeds in a small frying pan over low heat for 2–3 minutes, or until fragrant. Crush in a spice grinder, or mortar and pestle until it forms a fine powder. Transfer to a small bowl and mix with 2 teaspoons onion powder and ½ teaspoon salt.

mediterranean rub

Dry-fry 2 tablespoons coriander seeds, 1 tablespoon fennel seeds, 1 tablespoon cumin seeds and 2 teaspoons black peppercorns in a frying pan over medium heat for 2 minutes, or until fragrant. Cool and mix with 2 teaspoons dried rosemary, and ½ teaspoon salt, then grind in a spice grinder or mortar and pestle until a fine powder forms. Before using, mix with 2 cloves of crushed garlic.

moroccan rub

Place 1 teaspoon each of ground ginger, ground turmeric, paprika, ground nutmeg, ground cinnamon, ground cardamom, ground allspice and freshly ground black pepper in a small bowl and mix well.

storage hint

Any leftover spice mix can be stored in an airtight container for up to 6 months.

From left to right: Cajun rub, Cumin and coriander rub, Mediterranean rub, Moroccan rub.

lamb kofta curry

ingredients

- 1 1/4 cups (250 g/8 oz) jasmine rice
- 1 kg (2 lb) lean lamb mince
- 1 egg, lightly beaten
- 2 onions, finely chopped
- 120 g (4 oz) ready-made mild Korma curry paste
- 4 tablespoons chopped fresh coriander leaves
- 2 cloves garlic, crushed
- 2 tablespoons oil
- 400 g (13 oz) can chopped tomatoes

preparation: 15 minutes
cooking: 30 minutes
serves: 4

1 Preheat the oven to hot 220°C (400°F/Gas 6) and lightly grease two baking trays. Bring a large saucepan of water to the boil. Add the rice and cook for 12 minutes, stirring occasionally. Drain well.

2 Meanwhile, combine the mince, egg, 1 of the onions, 2 tablespoons of the curry paste, 3 tablespoons of the coriander, 1 clove of garlic and some salt. Form into balls, using 1 tablespoon of the mixture per ball, and place on one of the prepared baking trays.

3 Heat 1 tablespoon of the oil in a large non-stick frying pan over medium heat. Cook the balls in batches for 1 minute on each side, or until golden, but not cooked through. Put on the second baking tray and bake for 5–7 minutes, or until cooked through.

4 While the meatballs are baking, wipe the frying pan clean with paper towels, add the remaining oil and heat over medium heat. Add the remaining onion and garlic and cook for about 3 minutes, or until the onion has softened. Add the remaining curry paste and cook for 1 minute, before adding the tomato and 1 cup (250 ml/8 fl oz) water. Bring to the boil, then reduce the heat to low and simmer for about 10 minutes, or until the sauce thickens slightly. Season with salt.

5 Stir the meatballs and their juices into the sauce. Simmer for 5 minutes, or until the meatballs are warmed through. Serve with the steamed rice and sprinkle with the remaining coriander.

nutrition per serve
Fat 37.5 g; Protein 60 g; Carbohydrate 58 g; Dietary Fibre 6 g; Cholesterol 223.5 mg; 3405 kJ (810 Cal)

cooking hint

To avoid burning the rice, reduce the heat to as low as possible after bringing to the boil—a heat diffuser under the pan is ideal for this.

spring onion lamb with choy sum

ingredients

- 600 g (1 1/4 lb) lamb backstraps
- 1 tablespoon Chinese rice wine
- 1/4 cup (60 ml/2 fl oz) soy sauce
- 1/2 teaspoon white pepper
- 6 spring onions
- 1 1/2 cups (300 g/10 oz) long-grain rice
- 2 tablespoons oil
- 750 g (1 1/2 lb) choy sum, cut into 10 cm (4 inch) lengths
- 3 cloves garlic, crushed
- 1 tablespoon Chinese black vinegar
- 1 teaspoon sesame oil

preparation: 10 minutes + 10 minutes marinating
cooking: 30 minutes
serves: 4

1 Slice the lamb across the grain into very thin slices. Place in a non-metallic bowl with the rice wine, 1 tablespoon of the soy sauce, the white pepper and 1/2 teaspoon salt and mix well. Cover and refrigerate for 10 minutes. Slice the spring onions into 4 cm (1 1/2 inch) lengths on the diagonal.

2 Meanwhile, bring a large saucepan of water to the boil. Add the rice and cook for 12 minutes, stirring occasionally. Drain.

3 Heat a wok over high heat, add 2 teaspoons oil and swirl to coat. Add the choy sum, stir-fry quickly, then add 1 clove of the crushed garlic and 1 tablespoon of the soy sauce. Cook for 3 minutes, or until crisp but cooked. Immediately remove the greens and keep warm.

4 Wipe the wok clean with paper towels, then heat over high heat. Add 1 tablespoon oil and swirl to coat. Add the lamb in two batches and stir-fry quickly over high heat for 1–2 minutes, or until browned. Remove from the wok.

5 Add a little more oil to the wok, if necessary. Add the spring onion and remaining garlic and stir-fry for 1–2 minutes. Combine the vinegar, sesame oil and remaining soy sauce, then pour into the wok, stirring for 1 minute, or until combined. Return the lamb to the wok and continue to stir-fry for a minute, or until combined and heated through. Serve immediately with the choy sum and rice.

nutrition per serve
Fat 16 g; Protein 34 g; Carbohydrate 4 g; Dietary Fibre 3.5 g; Cholesterol 98 mg; 1260 kJ (300 Cal)

shopping tip

Chinese rice wine and Chinese black vinegar are available in Asian grocery stores.

rosemary lamb with baked vegetables

ingredients

- 3 cloves garlic, crushed
- 1 tablespoon fresh rosemary, chopped
- 2 teaspoons ground cumin
- 1/4 cup (60 ml/2 fl oz) olive oil
- 2 x 400 g (13 oz) trim lamb roasts, trussed
- 500 g (1 lb) orange sweet potato, peeled and cut into 3 cm (1 1/4 inch) cubes
- 500 g (1 lb) potatoes, unpeeled and cut into 3 cm (1 1/4 inch) cubes
- 250 g (8 oz) ready-made baba ganouj (eggplant dip)

preparation: 15 minutes + 1 hour marinating
cooking: 50 minutes
serves: 4

1 Place the garlic, rosemary, cumin and 1 tablespoon of the oil in a bowl, and mix together well. Coat the lamb in the mixture and marinate for 1 hour.

2 Preheat the oven to moderately hot 190°C (375°F/Gas 5). Heat 1 tablespoon of the oil in a large frying pan, add the meat and cook for 5 minutes, turning to brown on all sides. Place the lamb on a large baking tray. Toss the sweet potato and potato pieces in the remaining oil and sprinkle with some salt. Place on the baking tray with the lamb and bake for 20–25 minutes, or until the lamb is cooked to your liking. Remove the lamb, cover loosely with foil and keep warm. Return the vegetables to the oven for a further 15–20 minutes, or until nice and crispy.

3 To serve, remove the string from the lamb and cut into slices. Warm the baba ganouj slightly. Arrange the slices of lamb on four serving plates, top with a spoonful of baba ganouj and add a generous helping of the sweet potato and potato. Season to taste with salt and freshly ground black pepper and garnish with fresh rosemary sprigs, if desired.

nutrition per serve
Fat 34 g; Protein 55 g; Carbohydrate 37 g; Dietary Fibre 11 g; Cholesterol 132 mg; 2850 kJ (680 Cal)

cooking hint

Trussing is to tie the lamb up with kitchen string so that it not only holds its shape while cooking, it also cooks evenly. You can ask your butcher to do this for you.

ingredients

- 1/4 cup (60 ml/2 fl oz) oil
- 2 tablespoons Madras curry powder, or to taste
- 4 lamb fillets
- 1 tablespoon brinjal pickle, or to taste
- 250 g (8 oz) Greek-style plain yoghurt
- 350 g (11 oz) instant couscous
- 1/2 red capsicum, diced
- 4 spring onions, sliced on the diagonal

preparation: 15 minutes + 30 minutes marinating + 5 minutes standing
cooking: 20 minutes
serves: 4–6

1 Place 2 tablespoons of the oil and the curry powder in a bowl and mix well. Place the lamb in a non-metallic dish and brush the curry oil over it. Cover and marinate for 30 minutes. Preheat the oven to moderate 180°C (350°F/Gas 4).

2 Place the brinjal pickle and yoghurt in a bowl and mix together well. Add 2 tablespoons water and set aside. Heat the remaining oil in a frying pan, add the lamb and cook for 2–3 minutes on each side to seal. Transfer to an ovenproof dish and cook in the oven for 10–12 minutes. Remove from the oven and rest, covered, for about 5 minutes, then carve into slices.

3 Meanwhile, place the couscous in a bowl. Season with salt and cover with 450 ml (14 fl oz) boiling water. Stand for 5 minutes, or until all the liquid is absorbed. Fluff the couscous with a fork to separate the grains. Cool, then add the capsicum, spring onion and half the yoghurt mixture. Serve the lamb slices on a bed of couscous. Drizzle the remaining yoghurt mixture over the top. Garnish with fresh coriander, if desired.

nutrition per serve (6)
Fat 16 g; Protein 30 g; Carbohydrate 45 g; Dietary Fibre 3.5 g; Cholesterol 73 mg; 1881 kJ (450 Cal)

shopping tip

Brinjal pickle is made from eggplant and is widely available. Mango chutney or lime pickle can be used as substitutes.

sumac-crusted lamb fillets

ingredients

- 2 tablespoons olive oil
- 750 g (1½ lb) small new potatoes
- 2–3 cloves garlic, crushed
- ¼ cup (60 ml/2 fl oz) lemon juice
- 1 red capsicum, quartered lengthways
- 4 x 200 g (6½ oz) lamb backstraps
- 1 tablespoon sumac
- 3 tablespoons finely chopped fresh flat-leaf parsley
- 250 g (8 oz) ready-made baba ganouj (eggplant dip)

preparation: 15 minutes
cooking: 25 minutes
serves: 4

1 Heat the oil in a saucepan large enough to hold the potatoes in one layer. Add the potatoes and garlic, and cook, turning frequently, for 3–5 minutes, or until golden. Add the lemon juice and reduce the heat to medium–low. Simmer, covered, for 15–20 minutes, or until tender, stirring occasionally to prevent sticking. Remove from the heat. Season with salt and pepper.

2 Meanwhile, lightly oil a chargrill pan or barbecue plate and heat to very hot. Cook the capsicum pieces skin-side-down for 1–2 minutes, or until the skin starts to blister and turn black. Cook the other side for 1–2 minutes. Transfer to a plastic bag or bowl covered with plastic wrap and leave to cool slightly. Remove the skin and slice the quarters into thin strips.

3 Coat the lamb with sumac. Cook on the chargrill pan for 4–5 minutes on each side, or until cooked to your liking. Remove from the heat, cover with foil and rest.

4 Stir the parsley through the potatoes and season. Divide the baba ganouj among four plates. Cut the lamb into 1 cm (½ inch) slices on the diagonal and arrange on top of the baba ganouj with the capsicum strips. Serve with the potatoes and a salad, if desired.

nutrition per serve
Fat 18 g; Protein 47 g; Carbohydrate 29 g; Dietary Fibre 6 g; Cholesterol 130 mg; 1965 kJ (470 Cal)

shopping tip

Sumac is a Middle Eastern spice and is available from some gourmet food retailers and Middle Eastern grocery stores.

pan-fried lamb fillets with red wine sauce

ingredients

- 600 g (1¼ lb) small new potatoes
- 160 g (5½ oz) snow peas, trimmed
- 2 tablespoons olive oil
- 4 x 200 g (6½ oz) lamb backstraps, trimmed
- ⅔ cup (170 ml/5½ fl oz) red wine
- 1 tablespoon red currant jelly
- 2 teaspoons chopped fresh thyme
- 30 g (1 oz) butter, chilled and cut into cubes

preparation: 10 minutes
cooking: 20 minutes
serves: 4

1 Cook the potatoes in a large saucepan of lightly salted boiling water for 15–20 minutes, or until tender. Add the snow peas and cook for a further 1 minute. Drain the vegetables, return to the pan and toss gently with 1 tablespoon of the oil.

2 Meanwhile, heat the remaining oil in a large frying pan and cook the lamb backstraps over medium–high heat for 4–5 minutes, or until cooked but still pink in the middle. Remove from the pan, cover and keep warm.

3 Add the wine, red currant jelly and thyme to the pan and bring to the boil. Boil rapidly for 5 minutes, or until reduced and syrupy. Stir in the butter.

4 To serve, slice the lamb on the diagonal, divide among four plates and spoon some of the sauce on top. Serve with the potatoes and snow peas.

nutrition per serve
Fat 22 g; Protein 46 g; Carbohydrate 24 g; Dietary Fibre 4 g; Cholesterol 149 mg; 2130 kJ (510 Cal)

variation

You can use any vegetables you have on hand with this dish, such as broccoli, peas or sugar snap peas. It is also delicious with roasted vegetables, such as pumpkin and beetroot.

pork

asian pork salad

ingredients

- 2 teaspoons rice vinegar
- 1 small fresh red chilli, finely chopped
- 2 tablespoons soy sauce
- 1 teaspoon julienned fresh ginger
- 1/4 teaspoon sesame oil
- 1 star anise
- 2 teaspoons lime juice
- 250 g (8 oz) Chinese barbecued pork
- 100 g (3 1/2 oz) snow pea sprouts
- 2 spring onions, thinly sliced on the diagonal
- 1/2 red capsicum, thinly sliced

preparation: 15 minutes
cooking: 5 minutes
serves: 4

1 To make the salad dressing, place the vinegar, chilli, soy sauce, ginger, sesame oil, star anise and lime juice in a small saucepan and heat over medium–low heat. Stir together, then simmer gently for 2 minutes, or until just about to come to the boil. Remove the pan from the heat and allow to cool, then remove the star anise with tongs or a spoon.

2 Thinly slice the barbecued pork and place the slices in a serving bowl. Pick over the snow pea sprouts, discarding any brown or broken ones, and add them to the bowl with the pork. Sprinkle the spring onion and capsicum over the salad, pour on the dressing, toss together well, then serve.

nutrition per serve
Fat 10 g; Protein 17 g; Carbohydrate 10 g; Dietary Fibre 3.5 g; Cholesterol 39.5 mg; 810 kJ (195 Cal)

shopping tip

Chinese barbecued pork (otherwise known as char siu) is available from Chinese barbecue shops. Ask for the meat to be unsliced so that you can slice it as thinly as you like at home.

hoisin pork with stir-fried greens and ginger rice

ingredients

- 1¾ cups (250 g/8 oz) jasmine rice
- 500 g (1 lb) pork fillets, thinly sliced
- 1 tablespoon caster sugar
- 2 tablespoons oil
- ½ cup (125 ml/4 fl oz) white wine vinegar
- 1 cup (250 ml/8 fl oz) hoisin sauce
- 2 tablespoons stem ginger in syrup, chopped
- 1.25 kg (2½ lb) mixed Asian greens (bok choy, choy sum or Chinese spinach)

preparation: 15 minutes + 10 minutes standing
cooking: 35 minutes
serves: 4

1 Rinse the rice and place it in a large saucepan. Add 1¾ cups (435 ml/14 fl oz) water and bring to the boil. Cover with a lid, reduce the heat to very low and cook for 10 minutes. Remove from the heat and leave to stand, covered, for 10 minutes.

2 Meanwhile, place the pork in a bowl and sprinkle with the sugar. Toss to coat. Heat a wok over high heat, add 1 tablespoon oil and swirl to coat. Add the pork in batches and stir-fry for 3 minutes, or until brown. Remove. Add the vinegar to the wok and boil for 3–5 minutes, or until reduced by two-thirds. Reduce the heat, add the hoisin sauce and 1 tablespoon of the ginger, and simmer for 5 minutes. Season to taste.

3 Reheat the wok over high heat, add the remaining oil and swirl to coat. Add the greens and stir-fry for 3 minutes, or until crisp and cooked. Stir the remaining ginger through the rice, then press into four round teacups or small Asian bowls, smoothing the surface. Unmould the rice onto four serving plates, arrange the pork and greens on the side and drizzle the sauce over the top.

nutrition per serve
Fat 17 g; Protein 50 g; Carbohydrate 177 g; Dietary Fibre 20 g; Cholesterol 60 mg; 4523 kJ (1080 Cal)

shopping tip

Stem ginger is young ginger that has been preserved in syrup. It is available from supermarkets or Asian food stores.

caramel pork and pumpkin stir-fry

ingredients

- $1\frac{1}{4}$ cups (250 g/8 oz) jasmine rice
- 300 g (10 oz) butternut pumpkin, peeled
- 500 g (1 lb) pork fillet
- 2 cloves garlic, crushed
- 2–3 tablespoons peanut oil
- $\frac{1}{3}$ cup (60 g/2 oz) soft brown sugar
- $\frac{1}{4}$ cup (60 ml/2 fl oz) fish sauce
- $\frac{1}{4}$ cup (60 ml/2 fl oz) rice vinegar
- 2 tablespoons chopped fresh coriander leaves
- 1.25 kg ($2\frac{1}{2}$ lb) mixed Asian greens

preparation: 15 minutes
cooking: 20 minutes
serves: 4

1 Bring a saucepan of water to the boil. Add the rice and cook for 12 minutes, stirring occasionally. Drain well.

2 Cut the pumpkin into pieces roughly 2 x 4 cm ($\frac{3}{4}$ x $1\frac{1}{2}$ inch) and 5 mm ($\frac{1}{4}$ inch) thick. Thinly slice the pork fillet, then combine with the garlic and 2 teaspoons of the peanut oil. Season.

3 Heat a wok until very hot, add 1 tablespoon oil and swirl to coat the side of the wok. When just starting to smoke, stir-fry the pork in two batches for 1 minute per batch, or until the meat changes colour. Transfer to a plate. Add the remaining oil to the wok and stir-fry the pumpkin for 4 minutes, or until tender but not falling apart. Remove and add to the pork.

4 Combine the sugar, fish sauce, vinegar and $\frac{1}{2}$ cup (125 ml/4 fl oz) water in the wok and boil for 9 minutes, or until syrupy. Return the pork and pumpkin to the wok and stir for 1 minute, or until well coated and heated through. Stir in the coriander.

5 Place the Asian greens in a bamboo steamer over a saucepan of simmering water for 3 minutes, or until wilted. Serve with the stir-fry and rice.

nutrition per serve
Fat 15.5 g; Protein 38 g; Carbohydrate 73 g; Dietary Fibre 6 g; Cholesterol 119 mg; 2445 kJ (585 Cal)

cooking hint

It's important to keep the wok very hot at all times when cooking or the meat will begin to stew rather than sizzle.

sausages and mash with french shallot gravy

ingredients

- 1/3 cup (80 ml/2 3/4 fl oz) olive oil
- 200 g (6 1/2 oz) French shallots, peeled and thinly sliced
- 1 tablespoon plain flour
- 1/2 cup (125 ml/4 fl oz) red wine
- 1 1/2 cups (375 ml/12 fl oz) good-quality beef stock
- 1 tablespoon Dijon mustard
- 1.5 kg (3 lb) potatoes, chopped
- 150 g (5 oz) butter
- 8 thick, good-quality pork sausages
- 450 g (14 oz) green beans, top and tailed

preparation: 15 minutes
cooking: 25 minutes
serves: 4

1 To make the shallot gravy, heat 2 tablespoons of the oil in a large frying pan over medium heat. Add the shallots and cook for 5 minutes, stirring frequently, until the shallots soften and become transparent. Add the flour and cook for 30 seconds. Increase the heat to high, pour in the wine and and stock and bring to the boil. Reduce the heat to medium and simmer for about 10 minutes, or until the sauce thickens and reduces. Stir in the mustard, then reduce the heat to medium–low and simmer very gently until the sausages and mash are ready.

2 Meanwhile, cook the potato in a large saucepan of boiling water for 12–15 minutes, or until tender. Drain and return to the pan with 1 tablespoon of olive oil and 120 g (4 oz) of the butter. Mash with a potato masher until smooth and creamy, then season to taste.

3 While the potatoes are cooking, prick the sausages several times with a fork. Heat a large frying pan over medium–high heat, add a tablespoon of oil and the sausages. Cook for 10 minutes, or until cooked, turning to brown evenly.

4 Cook the beans in a saucepan of lightly salted water for 4 minutes, or until just tender. When ready to serve, whisk the remaining butter into the gravy and season. To serve, place a mound of mashed potato on four serving plates, top with 2 sausages each and the beans and gravy on the side.

nutrition per serve
Fat 83 g; Protein 32.5 g; Carbohydrate 62 g; Dietary Fibre 11.5 g; Cholesterol 195 mg; 4780 kJ (1140 Cal)

variation

If you can't find French shallots, you can use 250 g (8 oz) thinly sliced red onions instead. The onions will need about 5 minutes extra cooking time for them to become transparent.

low-fat asian pork stew

ingredients

- 2 teaspoons olive oil
- 2 cloves garlic, crushed
- 1 tablespoon julienned fresh ginger
- 1 teaspoon Sichuan peppercorns, crushed
- 1 star anise
- 800 g (1 lb 10 oz) pork fillet, cut into 3 cm (1¼ inch) cubes
- 1 cup (250 ml/8 fl oz) chicken stock
- 1 tablespoon soy sauce
- 1 tablespoon cornflour
- 2 teaspoons chilli bean paste
- 250 g (8 oz) Chinese broccoli (gai larn), cut into 4 cm (1½ inch) lengths

preparation: 20 minutes
cooking: 50 minutes
serves: 4

1 Heat the olive oil in a saucepan over high heat. Add the garlic, ginger, Sichuan peppercorns and star anise and cook for 30 seconds, or until fragrant. Add the pork and stir until coated in the spices.

2 Pour the stock, soy sauce and 1 cup (250 ml/8 fl oz) water into the pan and bring to the boil. Reduce the heat to low and simmer for 40 minutes, or until the pork is tender.

3 Combine the cornflour with 2 tablespoons of the cooking liquid, stirring until smooth. Add to the pan and stir over medium heat for 3–4 minutes, or until the mixture thickens slightly.

4 Stir in the bean paste and Chinese broccoli and cook for a further 2 minutes, or until the broccoli is just tender. Serve with steamed rice.

nutrition per serve
Fat 7 g; Protein 47 g; Carbohydrate 4 g; Dietary Fibre 3 g; Cholesterol 190 mg; 1135 kJ (270 Cal)

shopping tip

You can replace Chinese broccoli with regular broccoli or any other Asian green, such as bok choy. Asian greens are readily available at most fruit and vegetable shops, and many supermarkets.
Sichuan peppercorns and star anise are available at Asian food stores or in the spice aisle of some supermarkets.

japanese pork schnitzel curry

ingredients

1 tablespoon oil, plus extra for deep-frying
1 onion, cut into thin wedges
2 large carrots, cut into 2 cm (3/4 inch) cubes
1 large potato, cut into 2 cm (3/4 inch) cubes
60 g (2 oz) Japanese curry paste block, broken into small pieces
plain flour, for coating
4 x 120 g (4 oz) pork schnitzels, pounded to 4 mm (1/4 inch) thick
2 eggs, lightly beaten
150 g (5 oz) Japanese breadcrumbs (panko)

preparation: 25 minutes
cooking: 30 minutes
serves: 4

1 Heat the oil in a saucepan, add the onion, carrot and potato, and cook over medium heat for about 10 minutes, or until starting to brown. Add the curry paste and 2 cups (500 ml/16 fl oz) water and stir until the curry paste dissolves and the sauce becomes a smooth consistency. Reduce the heat and simmer for 10 minutes, or until the vegetables are cooked through. Season with some salt and freshly ground black pepper.

2 Season the flour well. Dip each schnitzel into the flour, shake off any excess and dip into the beaten egg, allowing any excess to drip off. Coat with the breadcrumbs by pressing each side of the schnitzel firmly into the crumbs on a plate.

3 Fill a deep heavy-based saucepan one-third full of oil and heat to 180°C (350°F), or until a cube of bread dropped into the oil browns in 15 seconds. Cook the schnitzels, one at a time, turning once or twice, for 5 minutes, or until golden and cooked through. Drain on crumpled paper towels.

4 Slice each schnitzel into about 5 pieces and serve with cooked rice. Ladle the curry sauce over the schnitzels. Garnish with fried onions and serve with pickles on the side, if desired.

nutrition per serve
Fat 22 g; Protein 38 g; Carbohydrate 40 g; Dietary Fibre 5 g; Cholesterol 150 mg; 2145 kJ (513 Cal)

shopping tip

This dish uses a lot of typically Japanese ingredients that are available at Asian food stores and large supermarkets. The Japanese breadcrumbs give an extremely light and crisp coating to fried foods, but you can use regular dry breadcrumbs instead.

baked mediterranean pork cutlets

ingredients

- 4 large pork loin cutlets, trimmed
- 2 tablespoons olive oil
- 2 cloves garlic, finely chopped
- 1 tablespoon finely chopped fresh rosemary
- 2 tablespoons fresh thyme
- 2 tablespoons balsamic vinegar
- 4 Roma tomatoes, halved lengthways
- 1 large red capsicum
- 4 small zucchini, trimmed and halved lengthways

preparation: 15 minutes + 20 minutes marinating
cooking: 45 minutes
serves: 4

1 Lightly grease a roasting tin. Arrange the pork cutlets in a single layer in the tin. Combine the olive oil, garlic, rosemary, thyme and 1 tablespoon of the balsamic vinegar, then spoon half the mixture over the pork cutlets. Season to taste with salt and freshly ground black pepper. Cover and marinate in the refrigerator for 20 minutes. Preheat the oven to hot 220°C (425°F/Gas 7).

2 Place 2 tomato halves, cut-side-down, on each chop and sprinkle the tomatoes with the remaining balsamic vinegar.

3 Remove the seeds from the capsicum and cut into 2 cm (3/4 inch) strips. Toss the capsicum and zucchini with the remaining herb mixture, then add to the dish around the cutlets. Bake for about 45 minutes, or until cooked through and well browned. Season with salt and freshly ground black pepper. Serve the pork cutlets with the roast vegetables and a crisp green salad.

nutrition per serve
Fat 17.5 g; Protein 43 g; Carbohydrate 4 g; Dietary Fibre 2.5 g; Cholesterol 116 mg; 1450 kJ (345 Cal)

cooking hint

Scrape the chop bones of any excess fat and sinew so that they don't burn during cooking. The presentation is also improved by doing this.

pork with paprika, potatoes and shallots

ingredients

- 1 tablespoon paprika
- 4 thick pork loin cutlets
- 2 tablespoons olive oil
- 1/4 cup (60 ml/2 fl oz) sherry vinegar
- 1/4 teaspoon cayenne pepper
- 1/2 cup (125 ml/4 fl oz) puréed tomatoes
- 400 g (13 oz) potatoes, cut into 2 cm (3/4 inch) cubes
- 8 French shallots, peeled
- 200 g (6 1/2 oz) rocket leaves

preparation: 15 minutes
cooking: 45 minutes
serves: 4

1 Put the paprika and 1/4 teaspoon each of salt and freshly ground black pepper in a small bowl and mix well. Sprinkle over both sides of the pork. Heat the oil over medium heat in a deep frying pan, large enough to fit the cutlets in a single layer, and cook the cutlets until brown on both sides.

2 Pour the sherry vinegar into the pan and bring to the boil, scraping the bottom of the pan to remove any sediment. Stir in the cayenne pepper, puréed tomato and 1 cup (250 ml/8 fl oz) hot water. Bring to the boil, then add the potato and shallots. Reduce the heat and simmer, covered, for 30 minutes, or until the sauce has thickened and reduced by half—check the liquid level once or twice, and add a little more water if necessary. Season with a little salt and pepper.

3 To serve, divide the rocket leaves among four serving plates and place a pork cutlet on top. Spoon the sauce and potatoes over the top.

nutrition per serve
Fat 17 g; Protein 41 g; Carbohydrate 17 g; Dietary Fibre 3.5 g; Cholesterol 103 mg; 1615 kJ (385 Cal)

variation

This dish is also delicious served on a bed of rice or buttered noodles to help soak up the rich juices.

perfect sauces for pork chops

PAN-FRIED PORK CHOPS

Choose a sauce from the adjacent recipes and read through the recipe before you start cooking the chops.

Lightly season four 180 g (6 oz) pork loin chops on the bone. Heat a heavy-based frying pan over medium heat. Add 1 tablespoon oil and 20 g (3/4 oz) butter to the pan. When the butter begins to foam, add the pork chops and cook for 5 minutes on each side, or until just cooked through. Remove from the pan and allow to rest in a warm place for 5 minutes, or while you make your sauce.

serves 4

apple and sage sauce

While the pork chops are cooking, peel and dice 4 Granny Smith apples. Put the diced apple in a small saucepan with 2 tablespoons sugar, 2 tablespoons white wine vinegar, 2 tablespoons water and a pinch of salt. Put a lid on the saucepan and simmer for about 10 minutes, or until the apple is pulpy, then stir in 2 tablespoons finely chopped fresh sage. Serve the sauce spooned over the pork chops.

creamy mustard sauce

Add 1 finely chopped red Asian shallot and 1 clove chopped garlic to the same pan you cooked the chops in. Sauté for 3 minutes, then add 1 cup (250 ml/8 fl oz) cream, 1/2 cup (125 ml/4 fl oz) chicken stock and 2 tablespoons Dijon mustard. Simmer over low heat for 8 minutes, or until thickened slightly. Season well, then add 1 1/2 tablespoons finely chopped fresh parsley. Serve with the sauce spooned over the pork chops.

orange sauce

In a small jug, mix together ½ cup (125 ml/4 fl oz) orange juice, ½ cup (125 ml/4 fl oz) chicken stock, 1½ teaspoons cornflour, 2 tablespoons orange marmalade and 2 teaspoons Marsala. Add the sauce to the pan you cooked the pork chops in and simmer, stirring, over low heat for 3 minutes, or until the sauce has thickened slightly. Add the segments from 1 orange and 1½ tablespoons of finely chopped fresh parsley. Season well with salt and pepper, return the chops to the pan and gently reheat, then serve.

soy and ginger sauce

Follow the basic recipe for the pork chops, but use ¼ teaspoon of sesame oil instead of the butter. In a small jug, mix together ¾ cup (185 ml/6 fl oz) chicken stock, 2 tablespoons salt-reduced soy sauce and 1 teaspoon cornflour. Add 1 teaspoon finely grated fresh ginger, 1 clove crushed garlic, and 1 finely chopped red Asian shallot to the pan you cooked the chops in. Sauté for 3 minutes, then add the stock mixture. Stir until the sauce boils and thickens. Season well with black pepper, return the chops to the pan and gently warm through. Serve, topped with 2 thinly sliced spring onions.

cooking hint

To test if the chops are cooked, pierce the meat with a skewer; if the juices run clear, the meat is cooked. Pork should always be completely cooked through to destroy any microscopic organisms that are sometimes found in raw pork.

From left to right: Apple and sage sauce, Creamy mustard sauce, Orange sauce, Soy and ginger sauce.

114 pork with prosciutto and oregano

ingredients

- 12 long sprigs fresh oregano
- 12 paper-thin slices prosciutto, folded in half lengthways
- 4 x 200 g (6½ oz) pork fillets, trimmed
- 2 tablespoons oil
- ½ cup (125 ml/4 fl oz) dry white wine
- 200 ml (6½ fl oz) chicken stock
- 2 tablespoons Worcestershire sauce

preparation: 15 minutes
cooking: 25 minutes
serves: 4

1 Preheat the oven to moderate 180°C (350°F/Gas 4). Carefully wrap 3 sprigs oregano and 3 slices prosciutto alternately around each pork fillet, securing with toothpicks.

2 Heat the oil in a non-stick frying pan, add the pork and cook over high heat, turning to brown on all sides. Transfer to an oven tray and bake for 10–15 minutes, or until cooked through.

3 Pour the white wine into the frying pan and bring to the boil, scraping the bottom of the pan to remove any sediment. Add the chicken stock and Worcestershire sauce and boil for 5 minutes, or until the sauce has reduced by half. To serve, remove the toothpicks and slice each pork fillet on the diagonal into 2 cm (¾ inch) thick slices. Arrange on four serving plates, then pour on the sauce. Delicious with mashed potato (see page 230) and green beans (see page 240).

nutrition per serve
Fat 20 g; Protein 9.5 g; Carbohydrate 1.5 g; Dietary Fibre 0 g; Cholesterol 30 mg; 1040 kJ (250 Cal)

variation

An alternative to the oregano is to use fresh sage leaves. You will need 4 medium sage leaves per fillet. Partially tuck the leaves under the slices of prosciutto so that they are exposed without being loose.

pork with plum sauce and choy sum

ingredients

- 600 g (1 1/4 lb) choy sum, cut into 6 cm (2 1/2 inch) lengths
- 1/2 cup (125 ml/4 fl oz) peanut oil
- 1 large onion, sliced
- 3 cloves garlic, finely chopped
- 2 teaspoons finely chopped fresh ginger
- 500 g (1 lb) pork loin, thinly sliced
- 2 tablespoons cornflour, seasoned with salt and pepper
- 1/4 cup (60 ml/2 fl oz) plum sauce
- 1 1/2 tablespoons soy sauce
- 1 teaspoon sesame oil
- 2 tablespoons Chinese rice wine

preparation: 15 minutes
cooking: 20 minutes
serves: 4

1 Bring a large saucepan of lightly salted water to the boil, add the choy sum and cook for 2–3 minutes, or until the stems are crisp but still tender. Plunge into iced water to chill completely, then drain well.
2 Heat a wok over high heat, add 1 tablespoon of the oil and swirl to coat. Add the onion, garlic and ginger and cook over medium heat for 3 minutes, or until softened. Remove from the wok.
3 Toss the pork in the seasoned cornflour to coat, shaking off any excess. Reheat the wok over high heat, add the remaining oil and swirl to coat. Add the pork in batches and cook for 3 minutes, or until golden brown on both sides. Remove from the wok.
4 Drain the oil from the wok and return the meat and any juices. Combine the plum sauce, soy sauce, sesame oil and sherry, and add to the wok. Cook over high heat for 2–3 minutes, then add the choy sum and return the onion mixture to the wok. Cook, stirring, for a further 2 minutes. Serve immediately with rice.

nutrition per serve
Fat 33 g; Protein 30 g; Carbohydrate 18 g; Dietary Fibre 3 g; Cholesterol 118.5 mg; 2070 kJ (495 Cal)

variation

If choy sum is not available, then use the same quantity of Chinese broccoli (gai larn) or any other leafy Chinese green, such as bok choy.
If Chinese rice wine isn't available, use dry sherry instead.

pork loin roast with apple walnut stuffing

ingredients

- 1/2 cup (50 g/1 3/4 oz) walnuts, chopped
- 1 green apple, peeled and cored
- 1/2 teaspoon ground cinnamon
- 2 tablespoons port
- 1.5 kg (3 lb) rindless, deboned, pork loin
- 100 ml (3 1/2 fl oz) maple syrup
- 8 parsnips, thinly sliced lengthways
- 500 g (1 lb) baby carrots
- 2 tablespoons oil

preparation: 15 minutes + 10 minutes standing
cooking: 1 hour 30 minutes
serves: 4

1 Preheat the oven to moderately hot 200°C (400°F/Gas 6). Grease a large roasting tin. Spread the nuts on a baking tray and grill under a medium–high grill for 2–3 minutes, or until lightly toasted.

2 Coarsely grate the apple and squeeze out the excess juice. Combine the apple, cinnamon, walnuts and port and season.

3 Unroll the pork loin, then spread the stuffing evenly over one-third of the loin lengthways. Re-roll the loin, tie securely and place, seam-side-down, in the prepared tin. Roast for 20 minutes. Reduce the heat to moderate 180°C (350°F/Gas 4). Baste the pork with some of the syrup and roast for 30 minutes.

4 Toss the parsnip, carrots and oil together in a large bowl. Add to the roasting tin around the pork and roast for a further 30–35 minutes, or until the vegetables are golden and tender. In the last 10 minutes of cooking, baste again with the syrup. Remove the pork from the tin, cover with foil and allow to stand for 10 minutes before slicing. Serve with the vegetables and any pan juices.

nutrition per serve
Fat 31 g; Protein 67 g; Carbohydrate 48 g; Dietary Fibre 8.5 g; Cholesterol 180 mg; 3098 kJ (743 Cal)

cooking hint

If you don't have port on hand red wine or apple cider work just as well.

ingredients

1 kg (2 lb) pork spareribs
125 g (4 oz) can puréed tomatoes
2 tablespoons honey
2 tablespoons chilli sauce
2 tablespoons hoisin sauce
2 tablespoons lime juice
2 cloves garlic, crushed
1 tablespoon oil

preparation: 15 minutes + 1 hour marinating
cooking: 20 minutes
serves: 4

1 Cut each sparerib into thirds, then lay in a single layer in a shallow non-metallic dish.

2 Mix together all the other ingredients, except the oil, and pour over the meat, turning to coat well. Cover with plastic wrap and refrigerate for 1 hour.

3 Preheat a barbecue grill and brush it lightly with oil. Drain the ribs, reserving the marinade, and cook them over medium heat, basting with the marinade, for 15–20 minutes, or until tender and browned, turning occasionally. Season to taste with salt and freshly ground black pepper, then serve hot with a green salad.

nutrition per serve
Fat 24 g; Protein 46 g; Carbohydrate 17.5 g; Dietary Fibre 2.5 g; Cholesterol 144 mg; 1965 kJ (470 Cal)

cooking hint

These ribs can also be baked in the oven. Place the drained ribs on a rack in a roasting tin and bake them in a moderate (180°C/350°F/Gas 4) oven for 45 minutes. Turn the ribs occasionally and baste with the marinade during cooking.

120 roast rack of pork with fig and marsala sauce

ingredients

300 g (10 oz) dessert figs
1/3 cup (80 ml/2 3/4 fl oz) Marsala
2 teaspoons Dijon mustard
1/2 cup (125 ml/4 fl oz) chicken stock
1.5 kg (3 lb) rack of pork, tied
120 ml (4 fl oz) oil
1 large red onion, sliced
18 fresh sage leaves
300 g (10 oz) green beans, trimmed

preparation: 10 minutes + 30 minutes soaking
cooking: 1 hour 40 minutes
serves: 4

1 Preheat the oven to very hot 240°C (475°F/Gas 9). Cut the figs into quarters, then combine with the Marsala, mustard and stock, and soak for 30 minutes.

2 With a sharp knife, score lines in the pork rind about 5 cm (2 inch) apart, brush with 2 tablespoons of the oil and season. Place in a large roasting tin, cook for 15 minutes, then reduce the heat to moderately hot 200°C (400°F/Gas 6). Add the onion and cook for 40 minutes. Add the fig mixture to the pan and cook for 30–40 minutes, or until the pork juices run clear when the thickest section is pierced with a skewer.

3 Meanwhile, heat the remaining oil in a small saucepan over high heat. Add the sage leaves a few at a time for 30 seconds per batch. Remove with a slotted spoon and drain on crumpled paper towels.

4 Remove the pork and onion from the oven and allow the meat to rest for 5 minutes. Drain off the excess fat from the tin. Reduce the sauce on the stovetop for 5 minutes, stirring to scrape up any sediment stuck to the bottom of the pan.

5 Cook the beans in a saucepan of boiling water for 4 minutes. Drain, season to taste and keep warm.

6 To serve, slice the pork into four portions, using the bones as a guide. Pour the sauce over the pork. Garnish with the fried sage leaves and serve with the beans.

nutrition per serve
Fat 28 g; Protein 51 g; Carbohydrate 20.5 g; Dietary Fibre 4 g; Cholesterol 142 mg; 2303 kJ (548 Cal)

shopping tip

Dessert figs can be found in the preserved fruit section of large supermarkets.

chinese barbecued pork and noodle soup

ingredients

- 1.25 litres chicken stock
- 3 spring onions, cut into 4 cm (1 1/2 inch) lengths
- 4 thin slices fresh ginger
- 1 tablespoon Chinese rice wine
- 1 tablespoon oyster sauce.
- 300 g (10 oz) thinly sliced Chinese barbecued pork fillet
- 2 cups (350 g/11 oz) roughly chopped bok choy
- 200 g (6 1/2 oz) fresh flat egg noodles
- sliced spring onion, to garnish
- oyster sauce, to serve

preparation: 10 minutes
cooking: 10 minutes
serves: 4

1 Pour the stock and 1 cup (250 ml) water into a large saucepan and bring to the boil, then reduce the heat to a simmer. Add the spring onion, ginger, Chinese rice wine and oyster sauce and simmer for 3–4 minutes before adding the pork. Continue to simmer for 4–5 minutes, then add the bok choy.

2 Meanwhile, bring a saucepan of lightly salted water to the boil and cook the noodles for 1 minute. Drain well and rinse under cold water, then divide the noodles among four deep bowls. When the bok choy is just wilted, remove it and the pork with a slotted spoon or tongs and divide evenly among the bowls. Cover with the broth. Sprinkle with a little spring onion, drizzle with some oyster sauce, then serve.

nutrition per serve
Fat 6.5 g; Protein 29 g; Carbohydrate 31 g; Dietary Fibre 2.5 g; Cholesterol 76 mg; 1280 kJ (305 Cal)

cooking hint

If you don't have Chinese rice wine on hand, you can substitute it with an equal quantity of dry sherry. Chinese barbecued pork (otherwise known as char siu) is available from Chinese barbecue shops. Ask for the meat to be unsliced so that you can slice it as thinly as you like at home.

spicy sausage stew

ingredients

- 2 tablespoons olive oil
- 8 Italian sausages (700 g/ 1 lb 6½ oz), cut into 4 cm (1½ inch) lengths
- 1 leek, thinly sliced
- 1 red capsicum, seeded and chopped
- 425 g (14 oz) can chopped tomatoes
- ½ cup (125 ml/4 fl oz) chicken stock
- 300 g (10 oz) can butter beans, rinsed and drained
- 1⅓ cups (245 g/8 oz) instant couscous
- 25 g (¾ oz) butter, melted
- fresh flat-leaf parsley, to garnish

preparation: 15 minutes
cooking: 50 minutes
serves: 4

1 Heat half the oil in a saucepan over medium heat, add the sausage and cook for 6 minutes, or until browned. Remove. Cook the leek in the remaining oil over low heat for 10–12 minutes, or until soft. Add the capsicum and cook for 1–2 minutes. Return the sausage to the pan and stir in the tomato and stock. Bring to the boil, then reduce the heat and simmer for 30 minutes. Add the beans, season and stir for 1–2 minutes, or until heated through.

2 Place the couscous in a bowl. Season with salt and cover with 1⅓ cups (350 ml/11 fl oz) boiling water. Stand for 5 minutes, or until all the liquid is absorbed. Fluff the couscous with a fork. Divide among four serving bowls and spoon on the stew. Garnish with the parsley.

nutrition per serve
Fat 56 g; Protein 30 g; Carbohydrate 55 g; Dietary fibre 9.5 g; Cholesterol 116 mg; 3522 kJ (840 Cal)

shopping tip

If you can't find Italian sausages, look for any fresh spicy pork sausages, such as chorizo.

pork chops with apple and red onion chutney

ingredients

- 125 g (4 oz) butter
- 2 small red onions, sliced
- 2 Granny Smith apples, peeled, cored, then cut into quarters and sliced
- 1/4 teaspoon ground cloves
- 1/3 cup (115 g/4 oz) honey
- 4 x 250 g (8 oz) pork loin chops
- 2 teaspoons oil
- 1/2 teaspoon caraway seeds
- 725 g (1 lb 7 oz) green cabbage, thinly shredded

preparation: 15 minutes
cooking: 30 minutes
serves: 4

1 To make the chutney, melt 50 g (1¾ oz) of the butter in a saucepan, then add the onion, apple, cloves and honey. Simmer, covered, for 10 minutes over low heat. Increase the heat to medium and cook, uncovered, for a further 20 minutes, or until the liquid is reduced to a thick chutney. Allow to cool.

2 Meanwhile, season the chops well on both sides with salt and pepper. Heat the oil and 50 g (1¾ oz) of the butter in a large frying pan and sauté the chops over medium–high heat for 6–8 minutes on each side, or until browned and cooked through. Remove the pan from the heat, leaving the chops to rest for 2 minutes.

3 Melt the remaining butter in a large saucepan, add the caraway seeds and green cabbage and cook, covered, over medium–low heat, tossing a few times with tongs, for 12 minutes, or until the cabbage is tender.

4 To serve, place a pork chop on each serving plate with the cabbage on the side. Dollop with a spoonful of chutney.

nutrition per serve
Fat 34 g; Protein 55 g; Carbohydrate 41 g; Dietary Fibre 8.5 g; Cholesterol 222 mg; 2885 kJ (690 Cal)

cooking hint

Leaving the pork to rest for a couple of minutes before serving allows the juices to settle and the meat to remain moist.

seafood

steamed fish with ginger

ingredients

- 4 x 350 g (11 oz) whole bream, scaled and cleaned
- 2 tablespoons julienned fresh ginger
- 1/4 cup (60 ml/2 fl oz) peanut oil
- 2–3 tablespoons soy sauce
- 6 spring onions, sliced on the diagonal
- 45 g (1 1/2 oz) fresh coriander sprigs

preparation: 10 minutes
cooking: 15 minutes
serves: 4

1 Make two diagonal cuts in the thickest part of each fish on both sides, then put in a lined bamboo or other large steamer. Cover and steam for 10 minutes, or until cooked (the fish will flake easily when tested with a fork).

2 Place each whole fish on a serving plate and scatter some of the ginger over the fish.

3 Heat the oil in a small saucepan over medium heat until the oil begins to smoke. Pour some hot oil over each fish. The oil will sizzle and splatter, so stand back a little (the oil must be very hot or the fish won't go crisp and may seem oily). Drizzle the soy sauce over the fish and garnish with spring onion and fresh coriander sprigs. Delicious served with steamed rice and bok choy (see page 240).

nutrition per serve
Fat 27.5 g; Protein 53 g; Carbohydrate 2 g; Dietary Fibre 1 g; Cholesterol 193 mg; 1950 kJ (465 Cal)

variation

You can also use whole snapper or flounder for this dish.

green fish curry

ingredients

1 tablespoon peanut oil
1 onion, chopped
1½ tablespoons green curry paste
1½ cups (375 ml/12 fl oz) coconut milk
700 g (1 lb 6½ oz) boneless firm white fish fillets, cut into bite-sized pieces
3 fresh kaffir lime leaves
1 tablespoon fish sauce
2 teaspoons grated palm sugar or soft brown sugar
2 tablespoons lime juice
1 long fresh green chilli, thinly sliced

preparation: 15 minutes
cooking: 15 minutes
serves: 4

1 Heat a wok until very hot, add the peanut oil and swirl to coat the side of the wok. When the oil has just started smoking, add the onion and stir-fry for 2 minutes, or until softened. Stir in the curry paste and stir-fry for 1–2 minutes, or until fragrant. Pour in the coconut milk, stir well and bring to the boil.

2 Add the fish pieces and kaffir lime leaves to the wok, reduce the heat to low and simmer, stirring occasionally, for 8–10 minutes, or until the fish is cooked through.

3 Stir in the fish sauce, palm sugar and lime juice. Scatter the chilli slices over the curry before serving with steamed rice.

nutrition per serve
Fat 29 g; Protein 39 g; Carbohydrate 4.5 g; Dietary Fibre 1 g; Cholesterol 123.5 mg; 1820 kJ (435 Cal)

cooking hint

Fish such as ling, ocean perch, bream, warhou or blue eye are ideal in this curry.
Kaffir lime leaves give a wonderful tangy flavour to soups and curries, but the leaves should not be eaten because they are quite tough. In many Asian countries, the lime leaves are served in the dish for aesthetic reasons and guests remove the leaves themselves. However, you may prefer to remove the leaves before serving.

128 tuna steak with olive mayonnaise and wedges

ingredients

- 3 large Pontiac potatoes, unpeeled and cut lengthways into 8 wedges
- 1 1/3 cups (350 ml/11 fl oz) olive oil
- 2 egg yolks, at room temperature
- 25 ml (1/4 fl oz) lemon juice
- 1/3 cup (40 g/1 1/4 oz) pitted black olives, finely chopped
- 200 g (6 1/2 oz) baby rocket leaves
- 1 tablespoon finely chopped fresh rosemary
- 4 x 200 g (6 1/2 oz) tuna steaks

preparation: 15 minutes
cooking: 50 minutes
serves: 4

1 Preheat the oven to moderately hot 200°C (400°F/Gas 6). Place the potatoes evenly in a roasting tin and toss in 2 tablespoons of the oil. Bake for 45–50 minutes, or until crisp and golden.

2 To make the mayonnaise, place the egg yolks in a food processor, adding 1/4 cup (60 ml/2 fl oz) of the oil drop by drop. With the motor running, pour in 3/4 cup (185 ml/6 fl oz) of the oil in a thin stream until the mixture thickens and turns creamy. With the motor still running, add 1 teaspoon of the lemon juice, season with salt and blend for 30 seconds. Stir in the olives, cover and refrigerate.

3 To make the salad, toss together the rocket, 2 tablespoons of the oil and 1 tablespoon of the lemon juice in a serving bowl.

4 Press the chopped rosemary into the tuna steaks. Heat 1 tablespoon of the oil in a large frying pan and sear the tuna steaks over medium–high heat for 2–3 minutes on each side, or until cooked to your liking. Serve with the potato wedges, rocket salad and a dollop of olive mayonnaise.

nutrition per serve
Fat 66 g; Protein 56 g; Carbohydrate 22 g; Dietary Fibre 3.5 g; Cholesterol 128 mg; 3755 kJ (895 Cal)

cooking hint

The tuna tastes best if it is cooked but still a little rare in the centre.
To save time, you can buy whole-egg mayonnaise and mix the olives through it.

aromatic snapper parcels

ingredients

- 1 cup (30 g/1 oz) loosely packed fresh basil, chopped
- 2 large cloves garlic, chopped
- 1 tablespoon lemon juice
- 1 teaspoon grated lemon rind
- 1/4 cup (60 ml/2 fl oz) olive oil
- 4 x 200 g (6 1/2 oz) skinless snapper fillets, trimmed and boned
- 500 g (1 lb) small new potatoes
- 20 fresh asparagus spears
- 12 yellow baby squash

preparation: 10 minutes
cooking: 20 minutes
serves: 4

1 Preheat the oven to moderately hot 200°C (400°F/Gas 6). Combine the basil, garlic, lemon juice, rind and 2 tablespoons of the olive oil. Season to taste.

2 Place a fillet in the centre of a sheet of foil large enough to fully enclose it. Season well. Smear the fillet with 2 teaspoons of the basil mixture, then wrap into a secure parcel. Repeat with the remaining fillets. Place on a baking tray and refrigerate until required.

3 Cook the potatoes in a large saucepan of boiling water for 15–20 minutes, or until they are tender when tested with the tip of a knife. Drain and keep warm. While the potatoes are cooking, brush the asparagus and squash with the remaining oil. Place on a baking tray and season with black pepper. Bake for 8–10 minutes, or until golden and tender.

4 About 10 minutes before the vegetables are ready, place the fish parcels in the oven and cook for 5–7 minutes, or until the flesh flakes easily when tested with a fork—check one of the parcels after 5 minutes.

5 To serve, place an opened parcel on each of the four serving plates with the vegetables. Season and garnish with extra basil, if desired.

nutrition per serve
Fat 17 g; Protein 49 g; Carbohydrate 22 g; Dietary Fibre 7 g; Cholesterol 122 mg; 1845 kJ (440 Cal)

variation

To cook these parcels on the barbecue, wrap the fish in a double layer of foil.
You can use ling fillets or tail pieces of a salmon fillet.

salmon with gremolata and creamy mash

ingredients

- 4 tablespoons chopped fresh flat-leaf parsley
- 3 teaspoons grated lemon rind
- 2 large cloves garlic, finely chopped
- 850 g (1 lb 11 3/4 oz) Pontiac or desiree potatoes, quartered
- 40 g (1 1/4 oz) butter, chopped
- 2/3 cup (170 ml/5 1/2 fl oz) hot milk
- 2 tablespoons extra virgin olive oil
- 4 x 200 g (6 1/2 oz) salmon fillets

preparation: 15 minutes
cooking: 15 minutes
serves: 4

1 To make the gremolata, place the parsley, lemon rind and garlic in a small bowl, and mix together very well.

2 Bring a large saucepan of lightly salted water to the boil, add the potato pieces and cook for 10 minutes, or until tender. Drain well. Return to the pan and mash until smooth with a potato masher, or push through a sieve. Add the butter and hot milk, and return to the heat, stirring with a wooden spoon until smooth and creamy. Season with salt and pepper.

3 Heat the oil in a heavy-based frying pan and add the salmon, skin-side-down. Cook over high heat for 2 minutes on each side, or until cooked to your liking. Spoon the mash onto four warmed serving plates and top with the salmon. Scatter the gremolata over the fish and serve immediately with lemon wedges, if desired.

nutrition per serve
Fat 32 g; Protein 24.5 g; Carbohydrate 30 g; Dietary Fibre 4 g; Cholesterol 100 mg; 2124 kJ (505 Cal)

variation

You can use any firm-fleshed white fish, such as bass, whiting or cod, adjusting the cooking times according to the thickness of the fish.

prawn laksa

ingredients

- 375 g (12 oz) dried rice vermicelli
- 2 tablespoons oil
- 1 kg (2 lb) raw medium prawns, peeled and deveined, with tails intact
- 2–3 tablespoons ready-made laksa paste
- 1.5 litres coconut milk
- 1 Lebanese cucumber, cut into 5 cm (2 inch) batons
- 150 g (5 oz) bean sprouts
- 3 spring onions, chopped into 5 cm (2 inch) lengths

preparation: 15 minutes + 5 minutes standing
cooking: 15 minutes
serves: 6

1 Place the vermicelli in a bowl, cover with boiling water and leave for 5 minutes, or until tender. Drain, rinse and drain again.

2 Heat a wok over high heat, add the oil and swirl to coat. Add the prawns in two batches and cook, stirring, for 2 minutes, or until just starting to change colour. Remove from the wok.

3 Add the laksa paste to the wok and cook, stirring, for 1–2 minutes, or until fragrant. Stir in the coconut milk and bring slowly to the boil. Reduce the heat and return the prawns to the wok. Heat through for 2–3 minutes. To serve, divide the vermicelli among six deep serving bowls. Add the cucumber, bean sprouts and spring onion to the bowls and ladle the hot liquid and prawns over the top. Serve immediately.

nutrition per serve
Fat 60 g; Protein 37 g; Carbohydrate 15 g; Dietary Fibre 1.5 g; Cholesterol 250 mg; 3302 kJ (790 Cal)

cooking hint

To avoid overcooking the prawns, be sure to add the prawns to the wok when the oil is very hot and just beginning to smoke. This way, they will not stew. Remove them when they are just beginning to change colour—they will finish cooking when returned to the wok with the laksa sauce.

baked fish with coconut and kaffir lime leavess

ingredients

2 stems lemon grass, white part only
8 fresh kaffir lime leaves
1 cup (250 ml/8 fl oz) thick coconut cream
2 tablespoons fish sauce
1/2 teaspoon garam masala
2 teaspoons grated fresh ginger
2 cloves garlic, crushed
2 tablespoons chopped fresh coriander
4 x 200 g (6 1/2 oz) blue eye fillets
2 x 2 cm (3/4 x 3/4 inch) piece galangal, sliced into 4 pieces
1 lime, cut into wedges

preparation: 15 minutes
cooking: 20 minutes
serves: 4

1 Preheat the oven to moderately hot 200°C (400°F/Gas 6). Finely chop one of the lemon grass stems. Quarter the other lengthways and bruise it with the back of a knife.
2 Finely shred four of the lime leaves and place in a bowl with the coconut cream, fish sauce, garam masala, ginger, garlic, coriander, and finely chopped lemon grass. Mix together thoroughly, add the fish and toss to coat well.
3 Place a piece of bruised lemon grass and a piece of galangal in the centre of four 30 cm (12 inch) long pieces of baking paper. Place a fish fillet on top, put 1 kaffir lime leaf on top of each fillet and spoon on 1/4 cup of the coconut mixture. Wrap up securely, then wrap each parcel in foil.
4 Place in a non-metallic baking dish and bake for 15–20 minutes, or until cooked through. Unwrap the fish, discard the lemon grass and galangal pieces and serve on a bed of rice with the remaining cooking juices. Garnish with the lime wedges.

nutrition per serve
Fat 17.5 g; Protein 43 g; Carbohydrate 3.5 g; Dietary Fibre 1.5 g; Cholesterol 118 mg; 1430 kJ (340 Cal)

shopping tip

Galangal is a rhizome related to ginger. It has a peppery flavour and pinkish colour. It is available from greengrocers. Don't worry if you can't find it—although it adds a delicate perfume to the dish, it can be omitted.

mild prawn curry

ingredients

- 50 g (1¾ oz) butter
- 1 onion, finely chopped
- 1 clove garlic, crushed
- 1½ tablespoons curry powder
- 2 tablespoons plain flour
- 2 cups (500 ml/16 fl oz) milk
- 500 g (1 lb) peeled and deveined raw medium prawns
- 1½ tablespoons lemon juice
- 2 teaspoons sherry, optional
- 1 tablespoon finely chopped fresh parsley

preparation: 15 minutes
cooking: 15 minutes
serves: 4–6

1 Heat the butter in a large saucepan. Add the onion and garlic, and cook for 5 minutes, or until softened. Add the curry powder, cook for 1 minute, then stir in the flour and cook for a further 1 minute.

2 Remove the pan from the heat, pour in the milk and stir until smooth. Return the pan to the heat and stir constantly until the sauce thickens. Simmer for 2 minutes, then stir in the prawns. Continue to simmer for a further 5 minutes, or until the prawns are just cooked.

3 Stir in the lemon juice, sherry and parsley and serve immediately with rice.

nutrition per serve (6)
Fat 12 g; Protein 38 g; Carbohydrate 9 g; Dietary Fibre 1.5 g; Cholesterol 280 mg; 1247 kJ (298 Cal)

cooking hint

Curry powders vary in intensity from brand to brand and from batch to batch. If you are using a new curry powder, start by adding 1 tablespoon and taste the curry before adding the remaining 2 teaspoons.

herbed butters for fish fillets

PAN-FRIED FISH FILLETS

To begin, make a flavoured butter from the adjacent recipes. About 10 minutes before it is ready, sift 2–3 tablespoons plain flour and a little salt and pepper onto a plate. Pat dry 4 white fish fillets with paper towels, then coat in the flour, shaking off the excess.

Heat about 3 mm (1/8 inch) olive oil in a large frying pan until very hot. Cook the fish over medium heat for 3 minutes on one side, or until browned and golden—the time will vary depending on the thickness of the fish. Reduce the heat to low, then turn, and cook for 2 minutes. To test whether the fish is cooked, slip a knife into the flesh; if the knife slips in easily, the fish is ready.

Remove from the pan and drain briefly on paper towels before placing on a baking tray with 2–3 slices of the flavoured butter and grilling until the butter melts.

serves 4

lemon and dill butter

Put 100 g (3 1/2 oz) chopped, slightly softened unsalted butter in a bowl and beat smooth with electric beaters. Add 2 tablespoons finely chopped fresh dill, 1/2 teaspoon finely grated lemon rind and 2 tablespoons lemon juice and beat until well combined. Spoon onto a piece of baking paper and shape into a 4–5 cm (1 1/2–2 inches) wide log, then roll up and twist the ends to seal. Refrigerate for at least 30 minutes, or until firm, then cut into 5 mm (1/4 inch) thick slices.

olive, anchovy and caper butter

Put 100 g (3 1/2 oz) chopped, slightly softened unsalted butter in a bowl and beat smooth with electric beaters. Add 2 teaspoons chopped capers, 4 chopped anchovy fillets and 1 tablespoon finely chopped green olives. Spoon onto a piece of baking paper and shape into a 4–5 cm (1 1/2–2 inches) wide log, then roll up and twist the ends to seal. Refrigerate for at least 30 minutes, or until firm then cut into 5 mm (1/4 inch) thick slices.

pesto butter

Place ½ cup (15 g/½ oz) fresh basil, 1 tablespoon each of pine nuts and grated Parmesan and 1 clove crushed garlic in the bowl of a food processor or blender and process until smooth. Transfer to a bowl and add 100 g (3½ oz) chopped, slightly softened unsalted butter and beat with a wooden spoon until well combined. Spoon onto a piece of baking paper and shape into a 4–5 cm (1½–2 inches) wide log, then roll up and twist the ends to seal. Refrigerate for at least 30 minutes, or until firm, then cut into 5 mm (¼ inch) thick slices.

sweet chilli and coriander butter

Put 100 g (3½ oz) chopped, slightly softened unsalted butter in a bowl and beat smooth with electric beaters. Add 1 tablespoon sweet chilli sauce, 1 tablespoon chopped fresh coriander leaves, ½ teaspoon grated fresh ginger, 1 teaspoon fish sauce and ½–1 teaspoon sambal oelek. Spoon onto a piece of baking paper and shape into a 4–5 cm (1½–2 inches) wide log, then roll up and twist the ends to seal the log. Refrigerate for at least 30 minutes, or until firm, then cut into 5 mm (¼ inch) thick slices.

cooking hint

You can use any type of fish, but your cooking time will vary—the thicker the fillet, the longer the cooking time. All of the butters can be wrapped tightly and stored in the refrigerator for up to 1 week, or in the freezer for 2–3 months.

From left to right: Lemon and dill butter, Olive, anchovy and caper butter, Pesto butter, Sweet chilli and coriander butter.

crab and spinach soba noodle salad

ingredients

- 1/4 cup (60 ml/2 fl oz) rice vinegar
- 1/2 cup (125 ml/4 fl oz) mirin
- 2 tablespoons soy sauce
- 1 teaspoon finely chopped fresh ginger
- 400 g (13 oz) English spinach
- 250 g (8 oz) fresh cooked crab meat
- 250 g (8 oz) soba noodles
- 2 teaspoons sesame oil
- 2 spring onions, finely chopped
- 1 sheet nori, cut into julienne strips

preparation: 15 minutes
cooking: 5 minutes
serves: 4

1 Place the rice vinegar, mirin, soy sauce and ginger in a small bowl and mix well.

2 Bring a large saucepan of salted water to the boil. Blanch the spinach for 15–20 seconds, then remove with a slotted spoon (reserve the water in the pan). Place the spinach in a bowl of ice-cold water for 30 seconds. Drain and squeeze out the moisture, then coarsely chop. Combine with the crab meat and 2 tablespoons of the rice vinegar mixture.

3 Return the water to the boil and cook the noodles for 5 minutes, or until just tender. Drain, then rinse under cold water. Toss with the sesame oil, spring onion and the remaining dressing. Divide the noodles among four individual serving bowls, top with the spinach and crab meat, scatter with nori, and serve.

nutrition per serve
Fat 3.5 g; Protein 20 g; Carbohydrate 49 g; Dietary fibre 4.5 g; Cholesterol 52.5 mg; 1245 kJ (295 Cal)

variation

Replace the fresh crab meat with cooked fresh prawns or yabbies cut in half lengthways.

ingredients

- 1/2 pineapple, core removed, finely diced
- 6 spring onions, thinly sliced
- 2 tablespoons finely shredded fresh mint
- 2 tablespoons lime juice
- 1/4 cup (60 ml/2 fl oz) olive oil
- 6 tablespoons ready-made Cajun spice mix
- 6 ling fillets
- 1/4 cup (60 g/2 oz) Greek-style plain yoghurt

preparation: 15 minutes + 20 minutes refrigeration
cooking: 15 minutes
serves: 6

1 Place the pineapple, spring onion and mint in a bowl. Season with freshly ground black pepper and mix together well. Just before serving, add the lime juice and 2 tablespoons of the oil and stir together thoroughly.

2 Put the Cajun spice mix in a dry frying pan and cook over medium heat for 1 minute, or until fragrant. Spread the spice mix out on a sheet of baking paper, then lightly coat both sides of the fish fillets, gently patting off any excess. Refrigerate for 20 minutes.

3 Heat a barbecue or chargrill pan to hot and lightly brush with the remaining oil. Cook the fish in two batches for 2–3 minutes on each side, depending on the thickness of the fish. Serve with a little yoghurt spooned over the top and the salsa on the side.

nutrition per serve
Fat 15 g; Protein 12 g; Carbohydrate 8 g; Dietary Fibre 2 g; Cholesterol 47 mg; 883kJ (199 Cal)

cooking hint

To make your own Cajun spice mix, combine the following spices: 1 tablespoon each of garlic powder, onion powder, cayenne pepper and dried thyme leaves, 1 teaspoon dried oregano, 3 teaspoons sea salt and 1 teaspoon freshly ground black pepper. Store any leftover mixture in a small airtight container.

stir-fried fish with ginger

ingredients

- 1 tablespoon peanut oil
- 1 small onion, thinly sliced
- 3 teaspoons ground coriander
- 600 g (1¼ lb) boneless white fish fillets (e.g perch), cut into bite-sized strips
- 1 tablespoon julienned fresh ginger
- 1 teaspoon seeded and finely chopped fresh green chilli
- 2 tablespoons lime juice
- 2 tablespoons fresh coriander leaves

preparation: 20 minutes
cooking: 15 minutes
serves: 4

1 Heat a wok until very hot, add the oil and swirl to coat the side of the wok. Add the onion and stir-fry for 4 minutes, or until it is soft and lightly golden. Stir in the ground coriander and cook for about 2 minutes, or until fragrant.

2 Add the fish, ginger and chilli to the wok and stir-fry for about 6 minutes, or until the fish is cooked through. Stir in the lime juice and season to taste with salt and freshly ground black pepper. Garnish with fresh coriander leaves and serve with steamed rice.

nutrition per serve
Fat 9 g; Protein 30 g; Carbohydrate 1 g; Dietary Fibre 0.4 g; Cholesterol 105 mg; 895 kJ (214 Cal)

variation

Add 250 g (8 oz) quartered baby bok choy or other chopped Asian greens to the wok when the fish is half cooked—it will only need a couple of minutes cooking until it wilts.

ingredients

- 250 g (8 oz) cooked prawns
- 6 eggs
- 6 spring onions, thinly sliced
- 2 tablespoons peanut oil
- 1 tablespoon soy sauce
- 1 tablespoon oyster sauce
- 2 tablespoons dry sherry
- 1 tablespoon rice vinegar
- 1 teaspoon sugar
- 2 teaspoons finely chopped fresh ginger
- 1 tablespoon cornflour
- 2 teaspoons chopped fresh coriander leaves

preparation: 15 minutes
cooking: 5 minutes
serves: 4

1 Peel the prawns and gently pull out the dark vein from the backs, starting at the head end. Finely chop the prawn meat.

2 Place the eggs, ½ teaspoon salt and ¼ teaspoon ground white pepper in a bowl and whisk. Add the prawns and spring onion.

3 Heat a wok until hot, add the oil and swirl to coat. Pour in the egg mixture and cook for 2 minutes, or until puffed up and brown underneath. Divide into four and turn over to cook the other side. Remove and keep warm.

4 Add the soy and oyster sauces, sherry, rice vinegar, sugar, ginger and ¾ cup (185 ml/6 fl oz) water to the clean wok. Stir over medium heat until the sugar has dissolved, then boil for 1 minute.

5 Put the cornflour in a small bowl, add 2 tablespoons water and stir until a paste forms. Stir into the sauce until it boils and thickens. Pour over the omelette and sprinkle with the coriander.

nutrition per serve
Fat 17 g; Protein 23 g; Carbohydrate 6 g; Dietary Fibre 0.5 g; Cholesterol 365 mg; 1175 kJ (280 Cal)

variation

Cooked prawns are an easy option for the omelette, but you can also use 150 g (5 oz) flaked crab meat or halved scallops.

smoked fish chowder

ingredients

- 500 g (1 lb) smoked fish
- 1 potato, cut into cubes
- 30 g (1 oz) butter
- 1 onion, chopped
- 3 rashers bacon, chopped
- 1 celery stick, sliced
- 2 tablespoons plain flour
- 2 cups (500 ml/16 fl oz) milk
- 1/2 cup (125 ml/4 fl oz) cream
- 3 tablespoons chopped fresh flat-leaf parsley

preparation: 10 minutes
cooking: 20 minutes
serves: 4

1 Place the fish in a large frying pan, cover with water and bring to the boil. Reduce the heat to low and simmer for 5–8 minutes, or until the fish flakes easily with the tines of a fork. Remove the fish from the water, reserving 1/2 cup (125 ml/4 fl oz) of the cooking liquid. Using two forks, flake the fish, carefully removing any bones and skin.

2 Cook the potato in a saucepan of lightly salted boiling water for 5–6 minutes, or until tender. Drain.

3 Melt the butter in a large saucepan, add the onion, bacon and celery, and cook, stirring, over medium heat for 2–3 minutes, or until the onion is soft. Sprinkle the flour over the mixture and cook for a further 1 minute.

4 Remove the pan from the heat and gradually stir in the milk and the reserved cooking liquid from the fish, stirring until smooth. Return to the heat and stir until the mixture boils and thickens. Stir in the potato, cream, fish and parsley, and heat through. Season to taste with salt and freshly ground black pepper. Ladle the chowder into four warmed soup bowls. Season with freshly ground black pepper.

nutrition per serve
Fat 25 g; Protein 22 g; Carbohydrate 15 g; Dietary Fibre 1.5 g; Cholesterol 90 mg; 1738 kJ (415 Cal)

cooking hint

Chowder is an American seafood soup usually made with clams, but there are many variations. In recipes using fish, the most commonly used type is smoked cod or firm white fish fillets.

As a variation, add a small drained can of corn kernels to the soup when adding the potato and fish.

sesame-coated tuna with coriander salsa

ingredients

4 tuna steaks
3/4 cup (115 g/4 oz) sesame seeds
100 g (3½ oz) baby rocket leaves

Coriander salsa

2 tomatoes, seeded and diced
1 large clove garlic, crushed
2 tablespoons finely chopped fresh coriander leaves
2 tablespoons virgin olive oil, plus extra for shallow-frying
1 tablespoon lime juice

preparation: 15 minutes + 15 minutes refrigeration
cooking: 10 minutes
serves: 4

1 Cut each tuna steak into three pieces—try to make them evenly sized. Place the sesame seeds on a sheet of baking paper. Roll the tuna in the sesame seeds to coat. Refrigerate for 15 minutes.

2 To make the coriander salsa, place the tomato, garlic, coriander, oil and lime juice in a bowl, and mix together. Cover with plastic wrap and keep in the fridge until ready to serve.

3 Fill a heavy-based frying pan to 1.5 cm (5/8 inch) with the extra oil and place over high heat. Add the tuna in two batches and cook for 2 minutes on each side (it should be pink in the centre). Remove and drain on crumpled paper towels.

4 To serve, divide the rocket among four serving plates and arrange the tuna over the top. Spoon the salsa on the side and serve immediately. Top with a teaspoon of chilli jam, if desired, and season to taste with salt and freshly ground black pepper.

nutrition per serve
Fat 36 g; Protein 26 g; Carbohydrate 2 g; Dietary Fibre 2 g; Cholesterol 45 mg; 1696 kJ (403 Cal)

shopping tip

When selecting tuna steaks, look for ones that have a minimum of sinew and blood line (a dark red–brown patch). Although this is harmless, when cooked it is texturally and aesthetically unpleasant. If you prefer your tuna cooked a little rarer, then select thicker steaks or cook for less time.

blue eye cutlets in a spicy tomato sauce

ingredients

- 4 x 250 g (8 oz) blue eye cutlets, 2.5 cm (1 inch) thick
- 1 1/4 cups (250 g/8 oz) long-grain rice
- 2 tablespoons oil
- 1 teaspoon coriander seeds, lightly crushed
- 1 teaspoon black mustard seeds
- 1 1/2 tablespoons sambal oelek
- 400 g (13 oz) can chopped tomatoes
- 1 teaspoon garam masala
- 300 g (10 oz) baby English spinach leaves

preparation: 5 minutes
cooking: 25 minutes
serves: 4

1 Preheat the oven to moderate 180°C (350°F/Gas 4). Pat the fish dry with paper towels.

2 Bring a large saucepan of water to the boil, add the rice and cook for 12 minutes, stirring occasionally. Drain well.

3 Meanwhile, heat 1 tablespoon of the oil in a saucepan over medium heat. When hot, add the coriander and mustard seeds—the mustard seeds should start to pop after about 30 seconds. Add the sambal oelek and cook for 30 seconds, then stir in the tomato and the garam masala. Bring to the boil, then reduce the heat and simmer, covered, for 6–8 minutes, or until the sauce thickens.

4 Heat the remaining oil in a large non-stick frying pan over medium heat. Add the cutlets and cook for 1 minute on each side, or until evenly browned but not cooked through. Transfer to a 28 x 18.5 cm (11 x 7 inch) ceramic baking dish. Pour the tomato sauce over the fish and bake, uncovered, for 10 minutes, or until the fish is cooked through.

5 Meanwhile, wash the spinach and put in a saucepan with just the water clinging to the leaves. Cook, covered, for 1 minute, or until the spinach has wilted. Serve the fish cutlets and sauce with the spinach and some steamed rice.

nutrition per serve
Fat 12 g; Protein 51 g; Carbohydrate 56 g; Dietary Fibre 4.5 g; Cholesterol 130 mg; 2245 kJ (535 Cal)

shopping tip

Sambal oelek is a hot paste made from fresh red chillies. If you can't find it, you can replace it with an equal quantity of chopped fresh red chillies.

barbecued chermoula prawns

ingredients

- 1 kg (2 lb) raw medium prawns
- 3 teaspoons hot paprika
- 2 teaspoons ground cumin
- 1 cup (30 g/1 oz) firmly packed fresh flat-leaf parsley
- 1/2 cup (15 g/1/2 oz) fresh coriander leaves
- 100 ml (3 1/2 fl oz) lemon juice
- 145 ml (5 fl oz) olive oil
- 1 1/2 cups (280 g/9 oz) couscous
- 1 tablespoon grated lemon rind
- lemon wedges, to serve

preparation: 15 minutes + 10 minutes standing
cooking: 10 minutes
serves: 4

1 Peel the prawns, leaving the tails and the heads intact. Gently pull out the dark vein from the backs, starting at the head end. Place the prawns in a large bowl. Dry-fry the paprika and cumin in a frying pan for about 1 minute, or until fragrant, then remove the pan from the heat.

2 Blend or process the spices, parsley, coriander, lemon juice and 1/2 cup (125 ml/4 fl oz) of the oil until finely chopped. Add a little salt and freshly ground black pepper. Pour on to the prawns and mix well, then cover and refrigerate for 10 minutes. Heat a chargrill pan or barbecue plate to hot.

3 To cook the couscous, bring 1 cup (250 ml/8 fl oz) water to the boil in a saucepan, then stir in the couscous, lemon rind, the remaining oil and 1/4 teaspoon salt. Remove from the heat, cover and stand for 5 minutes. Fluff the couscous with a fork, adding a little extra oil if needed.

4 Cook the prawns on the hot chargrill pan or barbecue plate for 3–4 minutes, or until cooked and pink, turning and brushing with extra marinade while cooking—take care not to overcook. Serve the prawns on a bed of couscous, with a wedge of lemon.

nutrition per serve
Fat 31 g; Protein 36 g; Carbohydrate 56 g; Dietary Fibre 1.5 g; Cholesterol 186 mg; 2705 kJ (645 Cal)

cooking hint

The prawns only need a very brief marinating time; any longer and the marinade will start to react with and 'cook' the prawn meat.

salmon with cucumber coleslaw

ingredients

- 1 Lebanese cucumber
- 200 g (6 1/2 oz) green cabbage, thinly sliced
- 1/3 cup (80 ml/2 3/4 fl oz) rice vinegar, plus 1 tablespoon extra
- 2 teaspoons sugar, plus 1/3 cup (90 g/3 oz) extra
- 1/4 cup (60 ml/2 fl oz) fish sauce
- 4 spring onions, thinly sliced
- 1 teaspoon sambal oelek
- 4 x 200 g (6 1/2 oz) salmon fillets
- 1 tablespoon oil
- 1/2 cup (15 g/1/2 oz) fresh coriander leaves

preparation: 20 minutes
cooking: 15 minutes
serves: 4

1 Cut the cucumber in half lengthways. Remove the seeds with a teaspoon and cut the flesh into very thin slices on the diagonal. Place in a large bowl with the cabbage.
2 Combine the vinegar, sugar and 1 teaspoon salt in a small saucepan and simmer over low heat until the sugar and salt have dissolved. Cool slightly, then pour over the cabbage mixture. Refrigerate.
3 Place the extra sugar and 2 tablespoons water in a small saucepan. Cook over medium heat for 5 minutes, shaking the pan occasionally, until the sugar melts and turns golden. Remove from the heat and add the fish sauce, spring onion, sambal oelek and remaining vinegar, .
4 Season the salmon lightly with salt. Heat a large frying pan over medium heat, add the oil, and then add the salmon and cook on one side for 1 minute, or until browned. Turn over and cook for 1 minute. Reduce the heat to medium and add the sauce. Thoroughly coat the salmon in the glaze.
5 Toss the coriander through the cabbage mixture, and season to taste. Put the salmon on top of the coleslaw and serve with rice.

nutrition per serve
Fat 19 g; Protein 42 g; Carbohydrate 28 g; Dietary Fibre 3 g; Cholesterol 104 mg; 1875 kJ (450 Cal)

cooking hint

The cooking times will give a medium result. Adjust the times for your preferred level of doneness.
If sambal oelek is unavailable, you can use an equal amount of chopped fresh red chillies.

salt and pepper squid

ingredients

- 1 cup (125 g/4 oz) cornflour
- 1 1/2 tablespoons salt
- 1 tablespoon ground white pepper
- 3 small fresh red chillies, seeded and chopped
- 1 kg (2 lb) cleaned squid tubes, sliced into rings
- 2 egg whites, lightly beaten
- oil, for deep-frying
- lime wedges, to serve

preparation: 15 minutes
cooking: 5 minutes
serves: 4

1 Combine the cornflour, salt, pepper and chilli in a bowl.
2 Dip the squid rings into the beaten egg white and then into the cornflour mixture. Shake off any excess cornflour.
3 Fill a heavy-based saucepan one-third full of oil and heat to 180°C (350°F), or until a cube of bread dropped into the oil browns in 15 seconds. Cook the squid in batches for 1–2 minutes, or until lightly golden all over. Drain on crumpled paper towels. Serve hot with steamed rice and some lime wedges.

nutrition per serve
Fat 5.5 g; Protein 40 g; Carbohydrate 27 g; Dietary Fibre 0.5 g; Cholesterol 448 mg; 1330 kJ (320 Cal)

cooking hint

The secret with squid is to cook it very briefly in a very hot pan so that it remains tender and doesn't become tough and rubbery. Remember that it will continue cooking once you have removed it from the pan.

STEAMED FISH FILLETS

Make the dressing or salsa of your choice from the adjacent recipes, then set it aside while you cook the fish fillets.

Pat dry 4 white fish fillets and season lightly on both sides with salt and freshly ground black pepper. Line a bamboo or metal steamer with baking paper and place over a large saucepan or wok one-third full of water—the base of the steamer basket should not be touching the water. If there is too much water, it will boil up into the food, if there is too little, the pan will boil dry. Bring the water to the boil, then place the fish fillets in the steamer, making sure there is enough room between them that they do not touch. Cover and steam for 8–10 minutes (the cooking time will vary according to the thickness of the fish), or until just cooked through and the flesh flakes easily with a fork. Remove from the steamer and serve with your salsa or dressing and steamed rice or a salad.

From left to right: Tomato and coriander salsa, Olive salsa, Ginger and spring onion dressing, Vietnamese dressing.

tomato and coriander salsa

Score a cross in the base of 4 vine-ripened tomatoes, then put in a large bowl of boiling water for 30 seconds. Plunge into cold water and peel the skin away from the cross. Cut the tomatoes in half crossways, scoop out the seeds with a teaspoon, then finely chop the flesh. Transfer the flesh to a bowl with 4 tablespoons roughly chopped fresh coriander leaves, 2 tablespoons each of rice vinegar and finely chopped red onion and 1 teaspoon caster sugar. Spoon over the warm fish.

olive salsa

Place ¾ cup (110 g/3½ oz) finely chopped pitted black olives, ¼ cup (40 g/1¼ oz) finely chopped red capsicum, 4 tablespoons finely chopped fresh mint, 2 tablespoons each of toasted sesame seeds and finely chopped French shallots and 1 tablespoon extra virgin olive oil in a bowl. Season with freshly ground black pepper and spoon over the warm fish.

ginger and spring onion dressing

Combine 2 tablespoons Japanese soy sauce, 1 tablespoon rice vinegar and 1½ tablespoons mirin in a small saucepan and simmer over low heat for 1 minute. Add 1 tablespoon julienned fresh ginger and 3 thinly sliced (on the diagonal) spring onions and simmer for another minute. Spoon over the warm fish.

vietnamese dressing

Combine ¼ cup (60 ml/2 fl oz) fish sauce, 2 tablespoons lime juice, 2 small cloves crushed garlic, 1–2 small seeded and sliced fresh red chillies, 2 teaspoons finely julienned carrot, 1 teaspoon sugar and 2 tablespoons water in a small bowl. Spoon over the fish or serve the sauce in a small bowl on the side.

152 baked trout with fennel and preserved lemon

ingredients

4 x 300 g (10 oz) whole fresh rainbow trout, cleaned
1 tablespoon extra virgin olive oil
2 spring onions, thinly sliced
1 small fennel bulb, thinly sliced
1/2 preserved lemon
1 tablespoon chopped fresh flat-leaf parsley
fennel fronds or flat-leaf parsley, to garnish

preparation: 15 minutes
cooking: 25 minutes
serves: 4

1 Preheat the oven to moderate 180°C (350°F/Gas 4). Lightly grease four large double squares of foil. Rinse the trout under cold water and pat dry with paper towels. Cut off the fins with scissors or a knife.
2 Heat the oil in a frying pan, add the spring onion and fennel, and cook, stirring occasionally, over low heat for 5 minutes, or until soft but not brown. Remove the pan from the heat. Remove the pulp and pith from the preserved lemon and discard. Thoroughly wash the rind and finely chop. Stir the rind and parsley into the fennel mixture, and season .
3 Spoon the fennel mixture into the fish cavities, pressing firmly to secure the filling. Place each fish on a square of foil and lay a few fennel fronds or parsley leaves on top. Firmly wrap each fish in foil and place on a baking tray. Bake for 20 minutes, or until cooked. Serve with mashed potato and steamed vegetables.

nutrition per serve
Fat 7 g; Protein 16 g; Carbohydrate 1 g; Dietary Fibre 1 g; Cholesterol 52 mg; 550 kJ (130 Cal)

serving tip

You can leave the trout in its foil and serve as is. Although it loses a little in the appearance stakes, the wonderful aromas that are released when the foil parcel is opened more than compensate.

salmon in ginger broth with bok choy and noodles

ingredients

2 teaspoons dashi powder
1 tablespoon julienned fresh ginger
8 spring onions, thinly sliced on the diagonal
750 g (1 1/2 lb) baby bok choy, trimmed, leaves separated
3 teaspoons Japanese soy sauce
200 g (6 1/2 oz) soba noodles
2 tablespoons peanut oil
6 salmon fillets (150–200 g/5–6 1/2 oz each), skin and bones removed

preparation: 10 minutes
cooking: 15 minutes
serves: 6

1 Place 1.5 litres water and the dashi powder in a large saucepan. Bring to the boil, and add the ginger, spring onion and bok choy. Reduce the heat and simmer, covered, for 5 minutes, or until the bok choy has wilted. Stir in the soy sauce, remove from the heat and keep warm.

2 Meanwhile, cook the noodles in a saucepan of boiling water for 1 minute, or until just tender. Drain and keep warm.

3 Heat the oil in a large frying pan, add the salmon fillets and cook for 3 minutes on each side, or until cooked to your liking. They should be rare in the middle. Divide the noodles among six serving bowls. Add the bok choy and spoon on the broth. Top with the salmon and season well. Serve sprinkled with coriander leaves and lime wedges, if desired.

nutrition per serve
Fat 20 g; Protein 21 g; Carbohydrate 8 g; Dietary Fibre 2.5 g; Cholesterol 0 mg; 1207 kJ (287 Cal)

shopping tip

Dashi is made from dried kelp (kombu) and dried fish (bonito) and is the basic stock used in Japanese cooking. It is available as granules or as a powder, both of which need to be dissolved in hot water. They are available from Asian food stores.

vegetarian

baked ricotta with ratatouille

ingredients

- 1.5 kg (3 lb) ricotta, well drained
- 4 eggs, lightly beaten
- 3 cloves garlic, finely chopped
- 2 tablespoons chopped fresh thyme
- 300 g (10 oz) eggplant, diced
- 1/3 cup (80 ml/2 3/4 fl oz) olive oil
- 3 capsicums, green, red and yellow, diced
- 425 g (14 oz) can chopped tomatoes

preparation: 15 minutes + 15 minutes standing
cooking: 1 hour 30 minutes
serves: 8

1 Preheat the oven to moderate 180°C (350°F/Gas 4). Put the ricotta, eggs, 1 finely chopped garlic clove and 1 tablespoon chopped fresh thyme in a bowl. Season and mix well. Pour the mixture into a lightly greased 22 cm (9 inch) springform tin and gently tap a couple of times on the bench to expel any air bubbles. Bake for 1½ hours, or until firm and golden. Cool on a wire rack, pressing down a few times to remove any air bubbles.

2 Meanwhile, make the ratatouille. Place the eggplant on a tray and sprinkle with some salt. Leave for 15 minutes, then rinse and dry with paper towels. Heat 2 tablespoons oil in a frying pan, add the eggplant and cook for 4–5 minutes, or until golden. Add the capsicum and remaining garlic, and cook for 5 minutes, adding an extra tablespoon of oil if necessary. Stir in the chopped tomatoes and remaining thyme, and cook for 10–15 minutes, or until rich and pulpy. Season.

3 Remove the ricotta from the tin and cut into wedges. Serve with a little ratatouille on the side, garnished with thyme sprigs

nutrition per serve
Fat 33 g; Protein 24 g; Carbohydrate 7 g; Dietary Fibre 2 g; Cholesterol 180 mg; 1768 kJ (422 Cal)

shopping tip

If possible, buy your ricotta from a delicatessen, where it is usually sold in wedges. It is far less watery that the ricotta sold in tubs at the supermarket and it requires minimal draining.

eggplant curry

ingredients

- 1 teaspoon ground turmeric
- 700 g (1 lb 6½ oz) slender eggplant, cut into 4 cm (1½ inch) rounds
- oil for deep-frying
- 2 tablespoons oil, extra
- 2 onions, finely chopped
- 2 tablespoons curry powder
- 2 cloves garlic, crushed
- 3 curry leaves, roughly chopped
- 1 cup (250 ml/8 fl oz) coconut cream

preparation: 20 minutes + 1 hour standing
cooking: 15 minutes
serves: 6

1 Mix together half the turmeric with 1 teaspoon salt and rub into the eggplant, ensuring the cut surfaces are well coated. Place in a colander and leave for 1 hour. Rinse and dry on crumpled paper towels.

2 Fill a deep, heavy-based saucepan one-third full of oil and heat to 180°C (350°F), or until a cube of bread dropped into the oil browns in 15 seconds. Cook the eggplant in batches for 1 minute, or until golden brown. Drain on crumpled paper towels.

3 Heat the extra oil in a large saucepan, add the onion and cook over medium heat for 5 minutes, or until browned. Add the curry powder, crushed garlic, curry leaves, eggplant and remaining turmeric to the pan, and cook for 2 minutes. Stir in the coconut cream and 1 cup (250 ml/8 fl oz) water, and season to taste with salt. Reduce the heat and simmer over low heat for 3 minutes, or until the eggplant is fully cooked and the sauce has thickened slightly. Serve hot.

nutrition per serve
Fat 15 g; Protein 3 g; Carbohydrate 6.5 g; Dietary Fibre 4 g; Cholesterol 0 mg; 715 kJ (170 Cal)

shopping tip

If slender eggplants are unavailable, use regular eggplants and cut them in quarters lengthways.
This is a fairly mild curry; if you would like to increase its heat, add ½ teaspoon of chilli powder when you add the curry powder.

162 mushroom and water chestnut stir-fry

ingredients

- 1/4 cup (60 ml/2 fl oz) oil
- 2 cloves garlic, crushed
- 1/2 cup (80 g/2 3/4 oz) pine nuts
- 750 g (1 1/2 lb) mixed fresh mushrooms (e.g. Swiss brown, oyster, shiitake), sliced
- 100 g (3 1/2 oz) snow peas, halved
- 230 g (7 1/2 oz) can sliced water chestnuts, drained
- 150 g (5 oz) bean sprouts
- 1/3 cup (80 ml/2 3/4 fl oz) oyster sauce
- 2 teaspoons sesame oil

preparation: 15 minutes
cooking: 10 minutes
serves: 4

1 Heat a wok over high heat, add 2 tablespoons of the oil and swirl around to coat the side of the wok. Add the garlic and pine nuts and cook, stirring constantly, for about 1 minute, or until the nuts turn light golden brown—be careful that they don't burn.

2 Add the mushrooms and stir-fry over high heat for 3 minutes. Add the snow peas and cook for a further 3 minutes, or until they are just tender, adding the remaining oil, if necessary.

3 Add the water chestnuts, bean sprouts, oyster sauce and sesame oil to the wok, and stir-fry for 30 seconds. Serve immediately with steamed rice.

nutrition per serve
Fat 31.5 g; Protein 13 g; Carbohydrate 16 g; Dietary Fibre 9 g; Cholesterol 0 mg; 1645 kJ (395 Cal)

cooking hint

If you like a bit of fire in your stir-fries, add 1–2 finely chopped fresh red chillies to the wok with the garlic and pine nuts.

nori omelette with stir-fried vegetables

ingredients

- 8 eggs
- 18 x 10 cm (7 x 4 inch) sheet nori
- 1/4 cup (60 ml/2 fl oz) oil
- 1 clove garlic, crushed
- 3 teaspoons finely grated fresh ginger
- 1 carrot, cut into thick matchsticks
- 2 zucchini, halved lengthways, sliced on the diagonal
- 200 g (6 1/2 oz) mixed mushrooms, larger ones sliced
- 1 tablespoon Japanese soy sauce
- 1 tablespoon mirin
- 2 teaspoons yellow miso paste

preparation: 15 minutes
cooking: 20 minutes
serves: 4

1 Lightly beat the eggs. Roll the nori up tightly and snip with scissors into very fine strips. Add to the eggs and season to taste with salt and pepper.

2 Heat a wok or heavy-based frying pan over high heat, add 2 teaspoons of the oil and swirl to coat the side of the wok. Add 1/3 cup (80 ml/2 3/4 fl oz) of the egg mixture and swirl to coat the base of the wok. Cook for 2 minutes, or until set, then flip over and cook for 1 minute. Remove and keep warm. Repeat with the remaining mixture, adding 2 teaspoons of the oil each time, to make four omelettes.

3 Heat the remaining oil in the wok, add the garlic and ginger and stir-fry for 1 minute. Add the carrot, zucchini and mushrooms in two batches and stir-fry for 3 minutes, or until soft. Return all the vegetables to the wok. Add the soy sauce, mirin and miso paste, and simmer for 1 minute. Divide the vegetables evenly among the omelettes, roll them up and serve immediately with rice.

nutrition per serve
Fat 24.5 g; Protein 17 g; Carbohydrate 4 g; Dietary Fibre 5 g; Cholesterol 375 mg; 1240 kJ (295 Cal)

shopping tip

The nori omelette uses some typically Japanese ingredients, which are available in Asian food stores or large supermarkets. See the glossary (page 292) for further information.

caramelized onion and parsnip soup

ingredients

- 30 g (1 oz) butter
- 3 large onions, halved and thinly sliced
- 2 tablespoons firmly packed soft brown sugar
- 1 cup (250 ml/8 fl oz) dry white wine
- 3 large parsnips, peeled, chopped
- 1.25 litres vegetable stock
- 1/4 cup (60 ml/2 fl oz) cream
- fresh thyme leaves, to garnish

preparation: 15 minutes
cooking: 40 minutes
serves: 4

1 Melt the butter in a large saucepan. Add the onion and sugar, and cook over low heat for 10 minutes. Add the wine and parsnip, and simmer, covered, for 20 minutes, or until the onion and parsnip are golden and tender.

2 Pour in the stock, bring to the boil, then reduce the heat and simmer, covered, for 10 minutes. Cool slightly, then place in a blender or food processor and blend in batches until smooth. Season. Drizzle with a little cream and sprinkle fresh thyme leaves over the top. Serve with toasted crusty bread slices.

nutrition per serve
Fat 13 g; Protein 4 g; Carbohydrate 23 g; Dietary Fibre 4 g; Cholesterol 40 mg; 1095 kJ (260 Cal)

cooking hint

If you prefer a thinner soup, add a little more stock. This soup will freeze well for up to 6 months. Make a double batch and freeze in single portions in ziplock bags. Thaw, bring to the boil and simmer briefly before serving.

polenta with mushrooms, spinach and tomatoes

ingredients

- 4 Roma tomatoes, halved lengthways
- 4 large field mushrooms
- 1/3 cup (80 ml/2 3/4 fl oz) garlic-flavoured oil
- 900 ml (29 fl oz) vegetable stock
- 175 g (6 oz) instant polenta
- 150 g (5 oz) goat's cheese, chopped
- 1/2 cup (50 g/1 3/4 oz) grated Parmesan
- 300 g (10 oz) baby English spinach leaves

preparation: 15 minutes
cooking: 20 minutes
serves: 4

1 Preheat the oven to moderately hot 200°C (400°F/Gas 6). Put the tomato and mushrooms in a non-metallic dish and brush with half the garlic oil. Transfer the tomato to a baking dish and bake for 20 minutes.

2 Meanwhile, place the stock in a large saucepan and bring to the boil, add the polenta in a slow steady stream and cook, stirring, for 10 minutes, or until creamy. Stir in the goat's cheese and half the Parmesan. Remove from the heat and keep warm.

3 Heat 1 tablespoon garlic oil in a frying pan, add the mushrooms and cook, turning once, for about 3 minutes, or until cooked, but not releasing too much juice. Remove from the pan. Add the remaining oil to the pan, add the spinach and cook for 3–4 minutes, or until just wilted. Spoon the polenta onto four warm serving plates, arrange the spinach on top, then a mushroom and top with two tomato halves. Sprinkle with the remaining Parmesan and serve.

nutrition per serve
Fat 33 g; Protein 18 g; Carbohydrate 33 g; Dietary Fibre 5 g; Cholesterol 40 mg; 2095 kJ (500 Cal)

cooking hint

To make your own garlic oil, marinate a crushed garlic clove in 1/3 cup (80 ml/2 3/4 fl oz) olive oil for 2 hours, then remove the garlic. Only make as much as you need because it does not keep.

steamed tofu with soy

ingredients

1 teaspoon sesame oil
2 tablespoons soy sauce
2 tablespoons kecap manis
500 g (1 lb) firm tofu, drained
1 1/2 teaspoons julienned fresh ginger
3 spring onions, thinly sliced on the diagonal
1 cup (50 g/1 3/4 oz) chopped fresh coriander leaves
ready-made fried garlic or crisp fried shallots, to garnish

preparation: 15 minutes + 30 minutes marinating
cooking: 10 minutes
serves: 4

1 Place the sesame oil, soy sauce and kecap manis in a bowl and mix together until well combined.
2 Cut the tofu in half widthways, then cut into triangles. Transfer to a plate and pour the sauce over the top. Marinate for 30 minutes, carefully turning the pieces once.
3 Sprinkle the julienned ginger over the tofu. Place the plate on a wire rack over a wok or large saucepan of simmering water. Cover with a lid and steam for 3–4 minutes before removing the lid and sprinkling with the spring onion and coriander. Return the lid to the wok and steam for a further 3 minutes. Remove from the heat and garnish with the fried garlic. Serve hot.

nutrition per serve
Fat 3.3 g; Protein 5 g; Carbohydrate 1 g; Dietary Fibre 0 g; Cholesterol 0 mg; 231 kJ (55 Cal)

shopping tip

Tofu comes in varying consistencies, each suitable for different cooking methods. For this recipe, it's important to buy firm tofu, which will stay intact during steaming. Read the label carefully when you are buying it to ensure you buy the correct kind of tofu.
Kecap manis can be replaced by soy sauce sweetened with a little soft brown sugar.

orange sweet potato, spinach and water chestnut stir-fry

ingredients

- $1\frac{1}{2}$ cups (300 g/10 oz) long-grain rice
- 500 g (1 lb) orange sweet potato
- 1 tablespoon oil
- 2 cloves garlic, crushed
- 2 teaspoons sambal oelek
- 227 g ($7\frac{1}{2}$ oz) can water chestnuts, sliced
- 2 teaspoons grated palm sugar
- 390 g (13 oz) English spinach, stems removed
- 2 tablespoons soy sauce
- 2 tablespoons vegetable stock

preparation: 15 minutes
cooking: 20 minutes
serves: 4

1 Bring a large saucepan of water to the boil. Add the rice and cook for 12 minutes, stirring occasionally. Drain well.

2 Meanwhile, cut the sweet potato into 1.5 cm (5/8 inch) cubes. Cook the sweet potato in a large saucepan of boiling water for 15 minutes, or until tender when pierced with the tip of a sharp knife. Drain well.

3 Heat a wok until very hot, add the oil and swirl to coat. Stir-fry the garlic and sambal oelek for 1 minute, or until fragrant. Add the sweet potato and water chestnuts and stir-fry over medium–high heat for 2 minutes. Reduce the heat to medium, add the palm sugar and cook for a further 2 minutes, or until the sugar has melted. Add the spinach, soy sauce and stock and toss until the spinach has just wilted. Serve with the rice.

nutrition per serve
Fat 5.5 g; Protein 10.5 g; Carbohydrate 82 g; Dietary Fibre 6.5 g; Cholesterol 0 mg; 1785 kJ (425 Cal)

shopping tip

Sambal oelek is made from mashed fresh red chillies mixed with salt and vinegar or tamarind. It is available in jars from the Asian section of large supermarkets.

barbecued vegetable skewers

ingredients

5 thin zucchini
5 slender eggplants
2 red capsicums
250 g (8 oz) kefalotyri cheese
12 button mushrooms
1/3 cup (80 ml/2 3/4 fl oz) lemon juice, plus 1 teaspoon grated rind
2 cloves garlic, finely chopped
5 tablespoons finely chopped fresh basil
145 ml (5 fl oz) olive oil
1 cup (185 g/6 oz) couscous
lemon wedges, to serve

preparation: 15 minutes + 30 minutes soaking + 10 minutes standing
cooking: 15 minutes
serves: 4

1 Soak 12 wooden skewers in water for 30 minutes. Cut the zucchini, eggplants, capsicums and cheese into 2 cm (3/4 inch) cubes. Halve the mushrooms.

2 Thread alternate vegetables and kefalotyri onto the skewers, then place them in a non-metallic dish in one layer.

3 Combine the lemon juice, garlic, 4 tablespoons of the basil and 1/2 cup (125 ml/4 fl oz) of the oil in a non-metallic bowl. Season. Pour two-thirds of the marinade over the skewers, reserving the rest. Turn the skewers to coat evenly, cover with plastic wrap and marinate for at least 5 minutes.

4 Put the couscous, lemon rind and 1 1/2 cups (375 ml/12 fl oz) boiling water in a large heatproof bowl. Stand for 5 minutes, or until all the water is absorbed. Add the remaining oil and basil, then fluff with a fork. Cover.

5 Meanwhile, heat a chargrill pan or barbecue plate to medium–high. Cook the skewers, brushing with any leftover marinade, for 4–5 minutes on each side, or until the vegetables are cooked and the cheese browns—take care that the cheese doesn't fall apart during cooking.

6 Divide the couscous and skewers among four plates. Season, then drizzle with the reserved marinade. Serve with lemon wedges.

nutrition per serve
Fat 51 g; Protein 23.5 g; Carbohydrate 41 g; Dietary Fibre 4 g; Cholesterol 56 mg; 2965 kJ (710 Cal)

cooking hint

Kefalotyri cheese is a very hard, scalded and cured sheep or goat's milk cheese with a mild flavour. Parmesan or pecorino can be substituted.

udon noodle stir-fry with miso dressing

ingredients

- 1 tablespoon white miso paste
- 1 tablespoon Japanese soy sauce
- 2 tablespoons sake
- 1/2 teaspoon sugar
- 400 g (13 oz) fresh udon noodles
- 1 tablespoon peanut oil
- 5 spring onions, cut into 5 cm (2 inch) lengths
- 1 red capsicum, thinly sliced
- 100 g (3 1/2 oz) fresh shiitake mushrooms, sliced
- 150 g (5 oz) snow peas, sliced lengthways into strips

preparation: 15 minutes
cooking: 10 minutes
serves: 4

1 Combine the miso paste with the soy sauce to form a smooth paste. Add the sake and sugar and mix together well.
2 Cook the noodles in a large saucepan of lightly salted boiling water for 1–2 minutes, or until tender and plump. Drain and rinse under cold water.
3 Heat the oil in a wok or large frying pan over high heat and swirl to coat the side of the wok. Add the spring onion and capsicum and toss frequently for 1–2 minutes, or until softened slightly. Add the mushrooms and snow peas and stir-fry for 2–3 minutes, or until they are tender.
4 Add the noodles and miso mixture to the wok and toss until combined and the noodles are warmed. Serve immediately.

nutrition per serve
Fat 5.5 g; Protein 8 g Carbohydrate 34 g; Dietary fibre 4 g; Cholesterol 0 mg; 925 kJ (220 Cal)

shopping tip

A number of traditional Japanese ingredients are used in this stir-fry, which are available either at Asian food stores or some large supermarkets. (Check the glossary on page 292 for information on these items.) If fresh shiitake mushrooms are unavailable, you can buy Swiss brown or oyster mushrooms instead.

170 asian noodle soup

ingredients

- 8 dried Chinese mushrooms
- 100 g (3½ oz) dried rice vermicelli
- 800 g (1 lb 10 oz) Chinese broccoli, cut into 5 cm (2 inch) lengths
- 8 fried tofu puffs, cut into strips
- 125 g (4 oz) bean sprouts
- 1 litre vegetable stock
- 2 tablespoons soy sauce
- 1½ tablespoons Chinese rice wine
- 3 spring onions, finely chopped
- fresh purple basil leaves, to serve

preparation: 20 minutes + 20 minutes soaking
cooking: 15 minutes
serves: 4

1 Place the dried mushrooms in a bowl, cover with boiling water and soak for 15 minutes. Drain, reserving ½ cup (125 ml/4 fl oz) of the soaking liquid. Squeeze the mushrooms to remove any excess liquid. Discard the stalks and thinly slice the caps.

2 Soak the dried rice vermicelli in a bowl of boiling water for 5 minutes. Drain well. Divide the vermicelli, broccoli, tofu puffs and bean sprouts among four serving bowls.

3 Place the reserved mushroom liquid, vegetable stock, soy sauce, wine, spring onion and mushrooms in a saucepan and bring to the boil. Cook, covered, for 10 minutes.

4 Ladle the soup into the serving bowls and garnish with the fresh basil leaves. Serve hot.

nutrition per serve
Fat 6.5 g; Protein 17 g; Carbohydrate 12 g; Dietary Fibre 13 g; Cholesterol 0 mg; 757 kJ (180 Cal)

variation

This soup has several ingredients that can be replaced with others. Try baby bok choy or choy sum instead of the Chinese broccoli, or dry sherry if you don't have any Chinese rice wine. Also, regular basil or Thai basil can be used instead of the rarer purple basil.

vegetable donburi

ingredients

- 2 cups (440 g/14 oz) short-grain white rice
- 10 g (1/4 oz) dried whole shiitake mushrooms
- 100 g (3 1/2 oz) green beans
- 5 spring onions
- 2 tablespoons oil
- 1 onion, sliced
- 2 slender eggplants, sliced on the diagonal
- 100 ml (3 1/2 fl oz) Japanese soy sauce
- 100 ml (3 1/2 fl oz) mirin
- 1/4 cup (60 g/2 oz) sugar
- 4 eggs, lightly beaten

preparation: 20 minutes + 15 minutes soaking
cooking: 35 minutes
serves: 4

1 Wash the rice and place in a saucepan with 2 1/2 cups (625 ml/20 fl oz) water. Bring to the boil, reduce the heat and simmer, covered, for 15 minutes. Leave, covered, for 10 minutes.

2 Soak the mushrooms in 1 2/3 cups (410 ml/13 fl oz) boiling water for 15 minutes. Meanwhile, cut the beans into 4 cm (1 1/2 inch) lengths and the spring onions into 2 cm (3/4 inch) lengths. Drain and reserve the liquid. Remove the stalks and cut the caps in half.

3 Heat the oil in a deep frying pan. Cook the onion over medium heat for 4 minutes. Add the eggplant and cook for 3–4 minutes, or until soft. Add the beans, mushrooms and spring onion and cook for 2–3 minutes, or until almost cooked. Combine the soy sauce, mushroom liquid, mirin and sugar, and stir through the vegetables. Simmer for 4 minutes.

4 Pour the egg over the vegetables, cover and simmer for 1 minute, or until partly cooked—the heat of the vegetables will continue to cook the egg. Serve the rice in bowls, spoon on the vegetable mixture and pour on the cooking sauce.

nutrition per serve
Fat 15 g; Protein 10 g; Carbohydrate 15 g; Dietary Fibre 4 g; Cholesterol 180 mg; 976 kJ (233 Cal)

storage hint

Japanese soy sauce is less salty and much lighter and sweeter than regular soy. Because it is naturally brewed it must be refrigerated after opening.

174 soy macaroni cheese

ingredients

- 500 g (1 lb) soy pasta twists
- 50 g (1¾ oz) soy spread
- 6 spring onions, thinly sliced
- 1 tablespoon soy flour
- 1 litre soy milk
- 2 tablespoons cornflour mixed into 2 tablespoons water
- 1 bay leaf
- 2½ cups (310 g/10 oz) grated Cheddar
- 1 teaspoon paprika
- 1 tablespoon finely chopped fresh parsley

preparation: 10 minutes
cooking: 30 minutes
serves: 4

1 Preheat the oven to moderately hot 200°C (400°F/Gas 6). Cook the soy pasta in a large saucepan of boiling water according to the packet instructions until *al dente*. Drain, and transfer to a large bowl.

2 Melt the soy spread in a saucepan over medium heat. Add the spring onion and cook for 1–2 minutes, or until soft. Add the soy flour and cook, stirring, for 2 minutes. Remove the pan from the heat and whisk in the soy milk and cornflour mixture until the sauce is smooth.

3 Return to the heat, add the bay leaf and bring to the boil, stirring constantly. Reduce the heat and simmer, stirring, for 3 minutes. Remove the bay leaf and stir in 2 cups (250 g/8 oz) of the cheese. Season well with salt and freshly ground black pepper. Pour the sauce over the pasta and mix together until well coated.

4 Spoon into a 3 litre ovenproof ceramic dish and sprinkle with the remaining cheese. Bake for 15 minutes, or until golden brown. Sprinkle with the paprika and parsley and serve immediately.

nutrition per serve
Fat 42 g; Protein 37 g; Carbohydrate 83 g; Dietary Fibre 17 g; Cholesterol 76 mg; 3583 kJ (856 Cal)

variation

Most short pasta shapes will work in the macaroni—try pasta shells or penne. Soy pasta is available in the health-food section of large supermarkets, but you can use wheat pasta instead.

ingredients

- 400 g (13 oz) potatoes, thinly sliced lengthways
- 60 g (2 oz) butter, melted
- 1½–2 teaspoons finely chopped fresh thyme
- 400 g (13 oz) pumpkin, thinly sliced
- 300 g (10 oz) zucchini (courgettes), thinly sliced lengthways
- 1 cup (250 ml/8 fl oz) Italian tomato passata
- ½ cup (50 g/1¾ oz) grated Parmesan

preparation: 15 minutes
cooking: 1 hour
serves: 4

1 Preheat the oven to warm 170°C (325°F/Gas 3). Lightly grease a 1.5 litre rectangular ovenproof dish. Combine the potato with one-third each of the butter and thyme. Season with salt and freshly ground black pepper, then place in the base of the prepared dish.

2 Mix together the pumpkin and another third of the butter and thyme. Season and press onto the potato. Combine the zucchini with the remaining butter and thyme. Season and press on to the pumpkin.

3 Spread the passata evenly over the top and cover with a piece of greased foil. Bake for 45 minutes, remove the foil and sprinkle with the grated Parmesan. Bake for a further 15 minutes, or until the top is golden brown and the vegetables are cooked through. Serve with a salad and crusty bread, if desired.

nutrition per serve
Fat 16.5 g; Protein 12 g; Carbohydrate 28 g; Dietary Fibre 7 g; Cholesterol 48.5 mg; 1305 kJ (310 Cal)

shopping tip

If you can't find tomato passata, use 1 cup of chopped fresh or canned tomatoes.

176 peanut and lime-crusted tofu with chilli jam

ingredients

- 1/4 cup (30 g/1 oz) besan (chickpea flour)
- 2 tablespoons soy flour
- 2 tablespoons soy sauce
- 2 tablespoons peanut butter
- 1 fresh kaffir lime leaf, finely shredded, plus extra, to garnish
- peanut oil, for deep-frying
- 500 g (1 lb) firm tofu, cut into 2 cm (3/4 inch) slices
- 600 g (1 1/4 lb) bok choy, quartered lengthways
- 1 tablespoon ready-made chilli jam

preparation: 15 minutes
cooking: 15 minutes
serves: 4

1 Combine the besan and soy flours, soy sauce, peanut butter, shredded lime leaf and 2 teaspoons salt in a bowl. Slowly add 100 ml (3 1/2 fl oz) water, stirring constantly, until the batter reaches a medium thick consistency.

2 Fill a large, heavy-based deep saucepan one-third full of oil and heat to 190°C (375°F), or until a cube of bread browns in 10 seconds. Quickly dip 2–3 slices of the tofu in the batter and deep-fry for 2 minutes, or until golden brown. Drain on crumpled paper towels and keep warm while you repeat with the remaining tofu slices and batter.

3 Steam the bok choy in a saucepan for 2–3 minutes, or until tender but still bright green. Divide the greens among the serving plates, arrange three pieces of tofu on top, dollop with a teaspoon of chilli jam and garnish with the extra shredded kaffir lime leaf.

nutrition per serve
Fat 24 g; Protein 24 g; Carbohydrate 8.5 g; Dietary Fibre 9.5 g; Cholesterol 0 mg; 1465 kJ (350 Cal)

shopping tip

Chickpea and soy flours are available from health food stores and the health food aisle of large supermarkets. Tofu is available in different consistencies. Check the label to ensure you are buying firm tofu—it holds its shape well.

bean enchiladas

ingredients

- 3 tomatoes
- 1 tablespoon olive oil
- 1 onion, thinly sliced
- 3 cloves garlic, crushed
- 1 fresh bird's-eye chilli, finely chopped
- 2 teaspoons ground cumin
- 1 tablespoon tomato paste
- 2 x 430 g (14 oz) cans three-bean mix
- 2/3 cup (20 g/3/4 oz) fresh coriander sprigs, 2 tablespoons chopped
- 8 flour tortillas
- 1 small avocado, chopped
- 1/2 cup (125 g/4 oz) light sour cream
- 2 cups (115 g/4 oz) shredded lettuce

preparation: 20 minutes
cooking: 25 minutes
serves: 4

1 Score a cross in the base of each tomato. Place the tomatoes in a large bowl of boiling water for 30 seconds, then plunge into cold water and peel the skin away from the cross. Cut the tomatoes in half crossways, then scoop out all the seeds with a teaspoon. Chop the tomato flesh.

2 Heat the oil in a deep frying pan over medium heat. Add the onion and cook for 3–4 minutes, or until just soft. Add the garlic and chilli and cook for a further 30 seconds. Add the cumin, chopped tomato, tomato paste and 1/2 cup (125 ml/4 fl oz) water and cook for 6–8 minutes, or until the mixture is quite thick and pulpy. Season to taste with salt and freshly ground black pepper.

3 Preheat the oven to warm 170°C (325°F/Gas 3). Drain and rinse the beans. Add the beans to the sauce and cook for 5 minutes to heat through, then add the chopped coriander.

4 Meanwhile, wrap the tortillas in foil and warm them in the oven for 3–4 minutes.

5 Place a tortilla on a plate and spread with 1/4 cup of the bean mixture. Top with some avocado, sour cream, coriander sprigs and lettuce. Roll the enchiladas up, tucking in the ends. Cut each one in half to serve.

nutrition per serve
Fat 23 g; Protein 17 g; Carbohydrate 47 g; Dietary Fibre 13.5 g; Cholesterol 20 mg; 1910 kJ (455 Cal)

shopping tip

Lebanese bread rounds or lavash bread will work just as well as the tortillas.

chinese broccoli with coconut rice

ingredients

- 1 tablespoon oil
- 2 stems lemon grass, white part only, bruised, cut into 5 cm (2 inch) lengths
- 1 clove garlic, crushed
- 2 teaspoons grated fresh ginger
- 1 cup (200 g/6½ oz) jasmine rice
- 1 cup (250 ml/8 fl oz) coconut milk
- 2–3 fresh kaffir lime leaves, crushed
- 800 g (1 lb 10 oz) Chinese broccoli, halved lengthways
- 2 tablespoons kecap manis
- 1 tablespoon lime juice

preparation: 10 minutes + 10 minutes standing
cooking: 30 minutes
serves: 4

1 Heat the oil in a saucepan over medium heat. Add the lemon grass, garlic and ginger and cook for 2 minutes, being careful not to burn the garlic. Add the rice and stir for about 2 minutes, or until it is well coated in the mixture.

2 Add the coconut milk, kaffir lime leaves and 2 cups (500 ml/16 fl oz) water to the pan and cover with a lid. Cook over low heat for 15–20 minutes, or until the rice is tender and all the liquid has been absorbed. Remove the pan from the heat and leave, covered, for 10 minutes.

3 Meanwhile, steam the Chinese broccoli until just wilted. Transfer to a platter and drizzle with the combined kecap manis and lime juice. Serve with the coconut rice.

nutrition per serve
Fat 16 g; Protein 14 g; Carbohydrate 42 g; Dietary Fibre 10 g; Cholesterol 0 mg; 1544 kJ (370 Cal)

cooking hint

To ensure that the rice cooks evenly, make sure you have a tight-fitting lid on the saucepan. A piece of foil wrapped around the bottom and side of the lid creates a secure seal. Remember not to stir the rice during cooking or it will become gluggy.

balti eggplant and tofu stir-fry

ingredients

- 2 tablespoons oil
- 1 onion, finely chopped
- 1/4 cup (70 g/2 1/4 oz) balti curry paste
- 300 g (10 oz) slender eggplant, cut on the diagonal into 1 cm (1/2 inch) slices
- 300 g (10 oz) firm tofu, cut into 1.5 cm (5/8 inch) cubes
- 3 ripe tomatoes, cut into wedges
- 1/4 cup (60 ml/2 fl oz) vegetable stock
- 75 g (2 1/2 oz) baby English spinach leaves
- 1/3 cup (50 g/1 3/4 oz) toasted cashew nuts

preparation: 15 minutes
cooking: 20 minutes
serves: 4

1 Heat a wok or deep frying pan until very hot. Add the oil and swirl it around to coat the side of the wok. Add the onion and stir-fry over high heat for 3–4 minutes, or until softened and lightly golden.

2 Stir in the balti curry paste and cook for 1 minute before adding the eggplant and cooking for 5 minutes. Add the tofu and gently toss for 3–4 minutes, or until it is nice and golden, taking care not to break up the tofu.

3 Add the tomato and stock and cook for 3 minutes, or until the tomato is soft. Stir in the spinach and cook for 1–2 minutes, or until wilted. Season to taste with salt and freshly ground black pepper. Sprinkle with cashews. This is delicious served with with saffron rice (see page 252).

nutrition per serve
Fat 20 g; Protein 10 g; Carbohydrate 10 g; Dietary Fibre 4.5 g; Cholesterol 1.5 mg; 1113 kJ (265 Cal)

cooking hint

You can use any Indian curry paste you like for this dish. If slender eggplants are unavailable, use the large, oval variety and cut them into 2 cm (3/4 inch) cubes.

180 ratatouille jacket potato

ingredients

8 large floury potatoes
olive oil, to rub, plus
2 tablespoons
1 small onion, finely diced
2 cloves garlic, crushed
1 small eggplant (200 g/
6½ oz), diced
1 red capsicum, seeded
and diced
1 zucchini, diced
½ teaspoon tomato paste
½ cup (125 g/4 oz) diced
tomatoes
½ cup (125 ml/4 fl oz)
vegetable stock
2 tablespoons of
shredded fresh basil
grated Parmesan, to
sprinkle

preparation: 15 minutes
cooking: 1 hour 30 minutes
serves: 4

1 Preheat the oven to moderate 180°C (350°F/Gas 4). Wash and dry the potatoes. Rub the skin with oil, and season with salt and freshly ground black pepper. Bake on the centre rack of the oven for 1½ hours, or until the skin is crisp and the flesh is tender when pierced with a skewer.

2 About 30 minutes before the potatoes are ready, heat the oil in a frying pan, add the onion and garlic and cook, stirring, for 5 minutes, or until softened. Add the diced eggplant, capsicum and zucchini and cook for 6–8 minutes over medium–high heat, or until the vegetables are tender. Reduce the heat to low, stir in the tomato paste, canned tomato and stock and simmer, covered, for 15 minutes. Season well, then stir in the basil.

3 Cut the top off the potatoes, scoop out the centre, then spoon in the ratatouille, sprinkle with grated Parmesan and serve.

nutrition per serve
Fat 14.5 g; Protein 6 g; Carbohydrate 24 g; Dietary Fibre 8.5 g; Cholesterol 0 mg; 1045 kJ (250 Cal)

cooking hint

For the best results when baking potatoes, use floury potatoes, such as King Edward or russet, or an all-purpose one, such as Pontiac.

roast pumpkin, pesto and feta pizza

ingredients

- 550 g (16 oz) pumpkin
- 2 cloves garlic, unpeeled
- 1 tablespoon olive oil, plus extra, for drizzling
- 4 x 23 cm (9 inch) Lebanese bread rounds
- 1/4 cup (60 g/2 oz) good-quality ready-made pesto
- 200 g (6 1/2 oz) crumbled feta
- 1 tablespoon pine nuts
- 2 cups (70 g/2 1/4 oz) rocket leaves

preparation: 15 minutes
cooking: 30 minutes
serves: 4

1 Preheat the oven to moderately hot 200°C (400°F/Gas 6). Lightly grease two baking trays. Cut the pumpkin into 1 cm (1/2 inch) dice, then toss with the garlic and olive oil in a roasting tin. Season well with salt and freshly ground black pepper, then bake for 15 minutes, or until tender.

2 Spread the Lebanese bread rounds with pesto, leaving a 1 cm (1/2 inch) border. Scatter with the pumpkin pieces, crumbled feta and pine nuts. Drizzle with a little extra oil. To cook, place the rounds on the prepared baking trays and bake for 15 minutes, or until the bases are nice and crispy.

3 When cooked, scatter with the rocket leaves, then serve.

nutrition per serve
Fat 33.5 g; Protein 32 g; Carbohydrate 94.5 g; Dietary Fibre 11 g; Cholesterol 36.5 mg; 3385 kJ (810 Cal)

variation

You can use almost any bread or pastry for the base of the pizza. Try two sheets ready-rolled shortcrust pastry and add an extra 5 minutes baking time. Two sheets are enough for a light meal for four people. Or, for a more traditional pizza, use two ready-made pizza bases and follow the packet instructions.

182 corn soup

ingredients

- 4 large ripe tomatoes
- 1$\frac{1}{2}$ cups (300 g/10 oz) corn kernels
- 2 tablespoons olive oil
- 2 cloves garlic, crushed
- 2 onions, chopped
- 3 cups (750 ml/24 fl oz) vegetable stock
- 1 tablespoon finely chopped fresh coriander leaves
- fresh coriander leaves, to garnish

preparation: 15 minutes
cooking: 30 minutes
serves: 4–6

1 Score a cross in the base of the tomatoes, then place in a bowl of boiling water for 30 seconds. Plunge into cold water and peel the skin away from the cross. Cut the tomatoes in half, scoop out the seeds with a teaspoon and chop the flesh.

2 Place half the corn in a food processor and, using a pulse action, process it until smooth. If necessary, scrape down the side of the bowl with a spatula to incorporate all the corn.

3 Heat the oil in a saucepan over medium heat, add the garlic and onion and cook for 5 minutes, or until softened. Reduce the heat to low, add the tomato and simmer gently for 10 minutes, stirring occasionally.

4 Add the stock, coriander, puréed corn and remaining corn kernels. Bring to the boil over high heat, then reduce the heat to low and simmer for 10 minutes, or until the soup has slightly thickened. Season to taste with salt and freshly ground black pepper. Ladle the soup into serving bowls, garnish with fresh coriander leaves and serve with bread rolls.

nutrition per serve (6)
Fat 7 g; Protein 2.5 g; Carbohydrate 12 g; Dietary Fibre 3.5 g; Cholesterol 0 mg; 500 kJ (120 Cal)

cooking hint

You can use fresh or canned corn for this recipe. If you are using fresh corn, remove the husk and silk, then remove the kernels by cutting down the length of the cob with a sharp knife.

rustic greek pie

ingredients

- 450 g (14 oz) packet frozen spinach, thawed
- 1 large sheet ready-rolled shortcrust pastry
- 3 cloves garlic, finely chopped
- 150 g (5 oz) haloumi cheese, grated
- 120 g (4 oz) feta, crumbled
- 1 tablespoon fresh oregano sprigs
- 2 eggs
- 1/4 cup (60 ml/2 fl oz) cream
- lemon wedges, to serve

preparation: 15 minutes
cooking: 30 minutes
serves: 4

1 Preheat the oven to moderately hot 200°C (400°F/Gas 6). Squeeze the excess liquid from the spinach.
2 Place the pastry sheet on a baking tray and spread the spinach in the middle, leaving a 3 cm (1 1/4 inch) border. Sprinkle the garlic over the spinach and pile the haloumi and feta on top. Sprinkle with oregano and season well with salt and freshly ground black pepper. Cut a short slit into each corner of the pastry sheet, then tuck each side of pastry over to form a border around the filling.
3 Lightly beat the eggs with the cream and carefully pour the egg mixture over the spinach filling. Bake for 25–30 minutes, or until the pastry is golden and the filling is set. Cut into four portions and serve with the lemon wedges and a green salad.

nutrition per serve
Fat 35 g; Protein 24 g; Carbohydrate 21 g; Dietary Fibre 6.5 g; Cholesterol 176 mg; 2050 kJ (490 Cal)

variation

If haloumi cheese is not readily available, use all feta instead. This pie is delicious served hot or cold.

tofu, snow pea and mushroom stir-fry

ingredients

- 1 1/4 cups (250 g/8 oz) jasmine rice
- 1/4 cup (60 ml/2 fl oz) peanut oil
- 600 g (1 1/4 lb) firm tofu, drained, cut into 2 cm (3/4 inch) cubes
- 2 teaspoons chilli paste
- 2 cloves garlic, finely chopped
- 300 g (10 oz) snow peas, trimmed
- 400 g (13 oz) mixed mushrooms, sliced
- 1/4 cup (60 ml/2 fl oz) kecap manis

preparation: 10 minutes
cooking: 15 minutes
serves: 4

1 Bring a large saucepan of water to the boil. Add the jasmine rice and cook for 12 minutes, stirring occasionally. Drain well.
2 Meanwhile, heat a wok over high heat until very hot. Add 2 tablespoons of the oil and swirl to coat the side of the wok. Add the tofu in two batches and stir-fry on all sides for 2–3 minutes, or until lightly browned, then transfer to a plate and set aside.
3 Add the remaining peanut oil to the wok and swirl around, then add the chilli paste, garlic, snow peas, mushrooms and 1 tablespoon water and stir-fry for 1–2 minutes, or until the vegetables are almost cooked but still crunchy.
4 Return the tofu to the wok, add the kecap manis and stir-fry for another minute, or until heated through and combined. Serve immediately with the steamed rice.

nutrition per serve
Fat 24 g; Protein 28.5 g; Carbohydrate 57 g; Dietary Fibre 10 g; Cholesterol 0 mg; 2315 kJ (555 Cal)

cooking hint

Firm tofu is used in this recipe because it will maintain its shape during cooking. Experiment with different mushrooms, such as shiitake, enoki or oyster, or a combination of all three.

vegetable tagine on couscous

ingredients

- 1/4 cup (60 ml/2 fl oz) olive oil
- 1 large red capsicum, seeded and quartered
- 1 large eggplant, cut into 1 cm (1/2 inch) rounds, then in half again
- 400 g (13 oz) can chopped Italian tomatoes
- 1 tablespoon harissa paste
- 1 tablespoon Moroccan spice blend
- 2 large zucchini, cut into 2 cm (3/4 inch) chunks
- 1 cup (250 ml/8 fl oz) vegetable stock
- 1 1/2 cups (225 g/7 oz) couscous
- 20 g (3/4 oz) butter

preparation: 10 minutes
cooking: 30 minutes
serves: 4

1 Heat 1 tablespoon of the oil in a saucepan over medium–high heat. Cook the capsicum, skin-side-down, covered, for 3–4 minutes, or until the skin is well browned. Remove from the pan. Peel off the skin and cut the flesh into 1 cm (1/2 inch) slices. Heat the remaining oil in the pan and cook the eggplant in batches over medium–high heat for 4–5 minutes, or until well browned. Remove.

2 Return the capsicum to the pan, then stir in the tomato, harissa paste and Moroccan spice blend. Pour in the stock and bring to the boil. Reduce the heat to medium–low and simmer for 15 minutes. Add the zucchini and eggplant and cook for a further 8 minutes, or until the vegetables are tender.

3 About 10 minutes before the vegetables are ready, place the couscous in a heatproof bowl with 1 1/2 cups (375 ml/12 fl oz) boiling water, and leave for 3–5 minutes. Stir in the butter and fluff with a fork until the butter has melted and the grains separate. Serve the tagine over the couscous.

nutrition per serve
Fat 19 g; Protein 11 g; Carbohydrate 52 g; Dietary Fibre 5.5 g; Cholesterol 13 mg; 1765 kJ (420 Cal)

shopping tip

Harissa is a hot Moroccan paste made from red chillies, garlic, salt and other spices. It is available from delicatessens in small tubes or jars.

mushroom pot pies

ingredients

- 100 ml (3½ fl oz) olive oil
- 1 leek, sliced
- 1 clove garlic, crushed
- 1 kg (2 lb) large field mushrooms, roughly chopped
- 1 teaspoon chopped fresh thyme
- 300 ml (9½ fl oz) cream
- 1 sheet ready-rolled puff pastry, thawed
- 1 egg yolk, beaten, to glaze

preparation: 15 minutes
cooking: 55 minutes
serves: 4

1 Heat 1 tablespoon of the oil in a frying pan over medium heat, add the leek and garlic and cook for 5 minutes, or until the leek is soft and translucent. Transfer to a large saucepan. Preheat the oven to moderate 180°C (350°F/Gas 4).

2 Heat the remaining oil in the frying pan over high heat and cook the mushrooms in two batches, stirring frequently, for 5–7 minutes per batch, or until the mushrooms have released their juices, are soft and slightly coloured. Transfer to the saucepan, then add the thyme.

3 Place the saucepan over high heat and pour in the cream, stirring well until thoroughly mixed. Cook, stirring occasionally, for about 8 minutes, or until the cream has reduced to a thick sauce. Remove from the heat and season well.

4 Divide the filling among four 1¼ cup (315 ml/10 fl oz) ramekins or ovenproof dishes. Cut the pastry into rounds slightly larger than the ramekins. Brush the edges of the dishes with a little of the egg yolk, place the pastry on top and press down to seal. Brush the tops with the remaining egg yolk and bake for 30–35 minutes, or until the pastry has risen and is golden brown. Great with mashed potato.

nutrition per serve
Fat 65 g; Protein 13.5 g; Carbohydrate 20 g; Dietary Fibre 7.5 g; Cholesterol 158 mg; 2970 kJ (710 Cal)

variation

To make one large pie, transfer the filling to a 20 cm (8 inch) ceramic pie dish or a 1.5 litre ovenproof dish. Brush the edge of the pie dish with a little of the egg yolk and place the pastry on top, pressing down around the edges. Trim the pastry and cook as directed.

thai sweet potato soup

ingredients

1 tablespoon peanut oil
2 onions, chopped
2 cloves garlic, chopped
2 teaspoons cumin seeds
1 small fresh red chilli, roughly chopped
1.5 kg (3 lb) orange sweet potato, peeled and roughly chopped
1.5 litres vegetable stock
275 ml (9 fl oz) coconut milk
fresh coriander leaves, to garnish

preparation: 10 minutes
cooking: 40 minutes
serves: 4–6

1 Heat the oil in a large saucepan, add the onion and cook for 1–2 minutes, or until softened. Stir in the garlic, cumin and chilli and cook, stirring, for 2 minutes. Add the sweet potato and cook for 2 minutes.

2 Pour in the stock, bring to the boil, then reduce the heat to low and simmer, partially covered, for 30 minutes, or until the sweet potato is tender when tested with the point of a sharp knife. Allow to cool slightly.

3 Transfer to a blender or food processor and blend in batches until smooth. Return to the saucepan over the heat, pour in the coconut milk and stir until warmed through. Ladle into serving bowls, garnish with coriander and serve.

nutrition per serve (6)
Fat 13 g; Protein 5.5 g; Carbohydrate 45 g; Dietary Fibre 6.3 g; Cholesterol 0 mg; 1335 kJ (320 Cal)

storage hint

Any leftover soup will freeze well in an airtight container for up to 6 months.

pasta & rice

190 pasta gnocchi with sausage and tomato

ingredients

- 500 g (1 lb) pasta gnocchi
- 2 tablespoons olive oil
- 400 g (13 oz) thin Italian sausages
- 1 red onion, finely chopped
- 2 cloves garlic, finely chopped
- 2 x 415 g (13 oz) cans chopped tomatoes
- 1 teaspoon caster sugar
- 35 g (1¼ oz) fresh basil, torn
- ½ cup (45 g/1½ oz) grated pecorino cheese

preparation: 15 minutes
cooking: 20 minutes
serves: 4–6

1 Cook the pasta gnocchi in a large saucepan of boiling water according to the packet instructions until *al dente*. Drain and return to the pan. Meanwhile, heat 2 teaspoons of the oil in a large frying pan. Add the sausages and cook, turning, for 5 minutes, or until well browned and cooked through. Drain on crumpled paper towels, then slice when they have cooled enough to touch. Keep warm.

2 Wipe clean the frying pan and heat the remaining oil. Add the onion and garlic and cook over medium heat for 2 minutes, or until the onion has softened. Add the tomato, sugar and 1 cup (250 ml/8 fl oz) water and season with pepper. Reduce the heat and simmer for 12 minutes, or until thickened and reduced a little.

3 Pour the sauce over the pasta and stir through the sausage, then the basil and half of the cheese. Divide among serving plates and serve hot, with the remaining cheese sprinkled over the top.

nutrition per serve (6)
Fat 29.5 g; Protein 17 g; Carbohydrate 29.5 g; Dietary Fibre 4 g; Cholesterol 57.5 mg; 1905 kJ (455 Cal)

shopping tip

Italian sausages are usually made with pork and either sage, fennel or rosemary. If they are not available, look for something similar with strong herb flavours.

ingredients

- 2 tablespoons olive oil
- 1 onion, finely chopped
- 2 cloves garlic, crushed
- 2 x 400 g (13 oz) cans chopped tomatoes
- 1/4 cup (60 g/2 oz) tomato paste
- 500 g (1 lb) spaghetti
- 500 g (1 lb) marinara mix
- 8 black mussels, beards removed, scrubbed
- 2 tablespoons shredded fresh basil

preparation: 15 minutes
cooking: 35 minutes
serves: 4–6

1 Heat the oil in a saucepan over medium heat, add the onion and cook for 5 minutes, or until softened and lightly browned. Add the garlic and stir for 1 minute, or until fragrant. Add the tomato and tomato paste and bring to the boil, then reduce the heat and simmer for 20–25 minutes, or until the sauce becomes rich and pulpy. Stir once or twice during cooking. Season with salt and freshly ground black pepper.

2 Meanwhile, cook the spaghetti in a large saucepan of boiling water according to the packet instructions until *al dente*. Drain well, return to the saucepan and keep warm.

3 Add the marinara mix and the mussels to the tomato sauce and cook for about 2–3 minutes, or until the seafood is cooked and the mussels are open. Discard any mussels that do not open. Stir in the basil. Toss the sauce through the warm pasta and serve.

nutrition per serve (6)
Fat 10 g; Protein 34 g; Carbohydrate 68.5 g; Dietary Fibre 6 g; Cholesterol 131 mg; 2125 kJ (510 Cal)

shopping tip

Marinara mix is a ready-made seafood mix available from most seafood stores. Alternatively, you can make your own by choosing a few different types of seafood, such as octopus, fish fillets and calamari and chop into bite-sized pieces.

192 risotto with scallops and minted peas

ingredients

1 litre chicken or vegetable stock
2¾ cups (360 g/12 oz) fresh or frozen baby peas
2 tablespoons sour cream
2 tablespoons finely shredded fresh mint, plus leaves, to garnish
1 tablespoon olive oil
1 small onion, finely chopped
2 cloves garlic, finely chopped
150 g (5 oz) arborio rice
16 large scallops (without roe)
1 tablespoon grated fresh Parmesan
lemon wedges, to serve

preparation: 15 minutes
cooking: 35 minutes
serves: 4–6

1 Pour the stock into a saucepan, bring to the boil, then add the peas. Simmer for 1–2 minutes, or until the peas are tender, then remove them with a slotted spoon and keep the stock at a low simmer. Blend 1¾ cups (230 g/7½ oz) of the peas with the sour cream in a food processor until smooth. Season with salt and pepper, then stir in 1 tablespoon of the mint.

2 Place the oil in a large saucepan and cook the onion over low heat for 4–5 minutes, or until just softened. Add the garlic and cook for 30 seconds before stirring in the rice to coat it in oil. Increase the heat to medium.

3 Add 1 cup (250 ml/8 fl oz) stock to the rice mixture and cook, stirring constantly, until all the liquid has evaporated. Add the stock, ½ cup (125 ml/4 fl oz) at a time until the rice is cooked and the mixture is creamy. This will take about 20 minutes.

4 Lightly season the scallops with salt and pepper. Heat a chargrill pan or hotplate, add the scallops and sear on both sides until cooked to your liking.

5 Fold the pea purée through the risotto with the reserved whole peas and Parmesan. Divide the risotto among the serving bowls and place the scallops on top. Sprinkle with the remaining mint, garnish with whole mint leaves and serve with a wedge of lemon to squeeze over the top.

nutrition per serve (6)
Fat 6 g; Protein 12.5 g; Carbohydrate 27.5 g; Dietary Fibre 4.5 g; Cholesterol 17 mg; 895 kJ (215 Cal)

cooking hint

Make sure the grill plate is very hot before searing the scallops to ensure that they become golden rather than stew in their own juices.

linguine with broccoli, pine nuts and lemon

ingredients

- 500 g (1 lb) linguine
- 600 g (1 1/4 oz) broccoli, cut into small florets
- 1/2 cup (80 g/2 3/4 oz) pine nuts
- 1/2 cup (125 ml/4 fl oz) extra virgin olive oil
- 2 teaspoons finely grated lemon rind
- 1/4 cup (60 ml/2 fl oz) lemon juice
- 1 teaspoon chilli flakes
- 1/3 cup (50 g/1 3/4 oz) finely grated good-quality Parmesan

preparation: 15 minutes
cooking time: 15 minutes
serves: 4–6

1 Cook the linguine in a large saucepan of boiling water according to the packet instructions until *al dente*. Drain well and return to the pan.

2 Meanwhile, bring a saucepan of water to the boil and cook the broccoli for 2 minutes, or until just tender but still bright green. Drain and set aside.

3 Heat a large, non-stick frying pan and toast the pine nuts for 2–3 minutes, or until just golden, shaking the pan to prevent them from burning. Remove from the pan and roughly chop. Reduce the heat to low, add the oil and lemon rind and gently heat until fragrant. Add the broccoli, chopped nuts, lemon juice and chilli and stir until warmed through. Season with salt and freshly ground pepper. Add to the pasta with the Parmesan and toss together well. Divide among serving bowls, then serve.

nutrition per serve (6)
Fat 27 g; Protein 19 g; Carbohydrate 60 g; Dietary Fibre 9 g; Cholesterol 8 mg; 2355 kJ (560 Cal)

variation

For a really fresh flavour, add 1/2 cup (30 g/1 oz) chopped fresh basil to the pasta when adding the Parmesan.

fettucine with cherry tomatoes, avocado and bacon

ingredients

- 4 cloves garlic, unpeeled
- 1/3 cup (80 ml/2 3/4 fl oz) olive oil
- 250 g (8 oz) cherry tomatoes
- 300 g (10 oz) short-cut bacon
- 350 g (11 oz) fresh fettucine
- 1 tablespoon white wine vinegar
- 2 tablespoons roughly chopped fresh basil
- 2 ripe avocados, diced
- whole fresh basil leaves, to garnish

preparation: 15 minutes
cooking: 25 minutes
serves: 4

1 Preheat the oven to moderately hot 200°C (400°F/Gas 6). Place the garlic at one end of a roasting tin and drizzle with 2 tablespoons of the olive oil. Place the tomatoes at the other end on the tin and season well. Bake for 10 minutes, then remove the garlic. Return the tomatoes to the oven for a further 5–10 minutes, or until soft.

2 Cook the bacon under a hot grill for 4 minutes on each side, or until crisp and golden. Roughly chop.

3 Meanwhile, cook the pasta in a large saucepan of boiling water until *al dente*. Drain well and transfer to a large bowl. Drizzle 1 tablespoon of the olive oil over the pasta and toss well. Season with salt and freshly ground black pepper and keep warm.

4 Slit the skin of each garlic clove and squeeze the garlic out. Place in a screw-top jar with the vinegar, chopped basil and remaining oil and shake well to combine.

5 Add the tomatoes and their juices, the bacon and the avocado to the fettucine, pour on the dressing and toss well. Garnish with the basil leaves and serve with a green salad and crusty bread, if desired.

nutrition per serve
Fat 44 g; Protein 27.5 g; Carbohydrate 50.5 g; Dietary Fibre 4 g; Cholesterol 106.5 mg; 2960 kJ (705 Cal)

shopping tip

Short-cut bacon is the meaty end of the bacon rasher and is also sold as eye bacon

ingredients

- 1.5 litres chicken or vegetable stock
- 2 tablespoons olive oil
- 100 g (3½ oz) butter, chopped
- 1 onion, finely chopped
- 650 g (1 lb 5 oz) small cap or Swiss brown mushrooms, stalks trimmed, sliced
- 3 cloves garlic, crushed
- ⅓ cup (80 ml/2¾ fl oz) dry white vermouth
- 2 cups (440 g/14 oz) arborio rice
- 1½ cups (150 g/5 oz) grated Parmesan

preparation: 10 minutes
cooking: 40 minutes
serves: 4–6

1 Bring the stock to the boil in a saucepan, then reduce the heat, cover, and keep at a low simmer.

2 Heat half the oil and 20 g (¾ oz) butter in a large saucepan over medium heat. Add the chopped onion and cook for 10 minutes, or until soft.

3 Heat the remaining oil and 40 g (1¼ oz) butter in a large frying pan over high heat. Add the mushrooms and garlic, and cook, stirring, for 10 minutes, or until soft and all the mushroom juices have been released. Transfer to a sieve over a bowl. Press down firmly with a spoon to extract all the juice. Season and set aside. Return the juices to the frying pan, add the vermouth and boil for 2 minutes, or until reduced to 1 tablespoon.

4 Add the rice to the onion mixture and stir for 1–2 minutes, or until well coated.

5 Add the mushroom juices and ½ cup (125 ml/4 fl oz) stock. Stir constantly over medium heat until all the liquid is absorbed. Continue adding more stock, ½ cup (125 ml/4 fl oz) at a time, stirring constantly for 20–25 minutes or until tender and creamy.

6 Remove from the heat, stir in the mushrooms, Parmesan and remaining butter. Season to taste.

nutrition per serve (6)
Fat 30 g; Protein 20 g; Carbohydrate 60 g; Dietary Fibre 5 g; Cholesterol 65 mg; 2496 kJ (596 Cal)

cooking hint

If you do not have dry vermouth, you can use a dry white wine instead.

penne with rustic lentil sauce

ingredients

1 litre chicken stock
1/3 cup (80 ml/2¾ fl oz) virgin olive oil, plus extra for drizzling
1 onion, chopped
2 carrots, diced
3 celery sticks, diced
3 cloves garlic, crushed
1 tablespoon plus 1 teaspoon chopped fresh thyme
400 g (13 oz) can lentils, drained and rinsed
350 g (11 oz) penne

preparation: 10 minutes
cooking: 30 minutes
serves: 4

1 Boil the chicken stock in a large saucepan for 10 minutes, or until reduced to 2 cups (500 ml/16 fl oz).
2 Heat 2 tablespoons of the oil in a large, deep frying pan, add the onion, carrot and celery and cook over medium heat for 10 minutes, or until browned. Add two-thirds of the garlic and 1 tablespoon of the thyme and cook for a further 1 minute. Pour in the stock, bring to the boil and cook for 8 minutes, or until reduced slightly and the vegetables are tender. Gently stir in the lentils until heated through.
3 Meanwhile, cook the pasta in a large saucepan of boiling water according to the packet instructions until *al dente*. Drain, return to the pan and toss with the remaining olive oil.
4 Stir the remaining garlic and thyme into the lentil sauce and season with plenty of salt and freshly ground black pepper—the stock should be slightly syrupy at this point. Transfer to a large bowl, add the pasta and mix thoroughly. Drizzle generously with virgin olive oil and serve with grated Parmesan, if desired.

nutrition per serve
Fat 18 g; Protein 16.5 g; Carbohydrate 72 g; Dietary Fibre 9 g; Cholesterol 0 mg; 2165 kJ (515 Cal)

cooking hint

If you wish to use dried lentils instead of canned, cover 1 cup (185 g/6 oz) washed brown lentils with 1 litre of water and a little salt. Bring to the boil, reduce the heat and simmer for 1 hour, or until the lentils are soft and most of the liquid has been absorbed.

ingredients

- 625 g (1 lb 5 oz) chicken ravioli
- 1 cup (50 g/1¾ oz) firmly packed fresh basil
- 2 cloves garlic, peeled
- ¼ cup (40 g/1¼ oz) pine nuts, toasted
- ½ cup (125 ml/4 fl oz) extra virgin olive oil
- 1 cup (100 g/3½ oz) grated Parmesan
- 3 tablespoons firmly packed fresh basil, extra, torn
- 30 g (1 oz) shaved Parmesan

preparation: 10 minutes
cooking: 10 minutes
serves: 4

1 Cook the chicken ravioli in a large saucepan of boiling water according to the packet instructions until *al dente*.

2 Meanwhile, blend the basil, garlic, pine nuts and olive oil in a food processor or blender until smooth. Stir in the Parmesan and season to taste with salt and freshly ground black pepper.

3 Drain the pasta, reserving 1 tablespoon of the cooking water to add to the pesto. Carefully toss the ravioli in the pesto and reserved water and finish with a drizzle of extra virgin olive oil, a little torn basil and some Parmesan shavings.

nutrition per serve
Fat 54 g; Protein 30 g Carbohydrate 57.5 g; Dietary Fibre 6.5 g; Cholesterol 83 mg; 3490 kJ (835 Cal)

storage hint

Pesto will freeze well for up to 6 months in an airtight container.
Pesto is traditionally served with spaghetti but is so versatile it can be used with any of your favourite pastas.

zucchini pasta bake

ingredients

- 200 g (6½ oz) risoni
- 40 g (1¼ oz) butter
- 4 spring onions, thinly sliced
- 400 g (13 oz) zucchini, grated
- 4 eggs
- ½ cup (125 ml/4 fl oz) cream
- 100 g (3½ oz) ricotta
- ⅔ cup (100 g/3½ oz) grated mozzarella
- ¾ cup (75 g/2½ oz) grated Parmesan

preparation: 15 minutes
cooking: 40 minutes
serves: 4

1 Preheat the oven to moderate 180°C (350°F/Gas 4). Cook the risoni in a large saucepan of boiling water according to the packet instructions until *al dente*. Drain well.

2 Meanwhile, heat the butter in a frying pan, add the spring onion and cook for 1 minute, then add the zucchini and cook for a further 4 minutes, or until softened. Cool slightly.

3 Place the eggs, cream, ricotta, mozzarella, risoni and half of the Parmesan in a bowl and mix together well. Stir in the zucchini mixture, then season with salt and black pepper. Spoon the mixture into four 2-cup (500 ml/16 fl oz) greased ovenproof dishes, but do not fill to the brim. Sprinkle with the remaining Parmesan and cook for 25–30 minutes, or until firm and golden brown on top.

nutrition per serve
Fat 41 g; Protein 28.5 g; Carbohydrate 39 g; Dietary Fibre 4.5 g; Cholesterol 311 mg; 2635 kJ (630 Cal)

shopping tip

Risoni is a small pasta that looks very similar to rice. It is preferable to buy a wedge of ricotta from a delicatessen rather than a tub from a supermarket because it is less watery and has a much better flavour.

penne with veal ragout

ingredients

- 2 onions, sliced
- 2 bay leaves, crushed
- 1.5 kg (3 lb) veal shin, cut into osso buco pieces
- 1 cup (250 ml/8 fl oz) red wine
- 2 x 400 g (13 oz) cans chopped tomatoes
- 1½ cups (375 ml/12 fl oz) beef stock
- 2 teaspoons chopped fresh rosemary
- 400 g (13 oz) penne
- 1 cup (140 g/4½ oz) frozen peas

preparation: 15 minutes
cooking: 2 hours 40 minutes
serves: 4

1 Preheat the oven to hot 220°C (425°F/Gas 7). Scatter the onion over the base of a large roasting tin, lightly spray with oil and place the bay leaves and veal pieces on top. Season with salt and pepper. Roast for 10–15 minutes, or until the veal is browned. Watch the onion to make sure that it doesn't burn.

2 Pour the wine over the veal and return to the oven for 5 minutes. Reduce the heat to moderate 180°C (350°F/Gas 4), remove the tin from the oven and pour on the tomato, stock and 1 teaspoon of the rosemary. Cover with foil and return to the oven. Cook for 2 hours, or until the veal is starting to fall off the bone. Remove the foil and cook for a further 15 minutes, or until the meat has loosened away from the bone and the liquid has evaporated slightly.

3 Cook the penne in a large saucepan of boiling water, according to the packet instructions, until *al dente*. Meanwhile, remove the roasting tin from the oven and allow the veal mixture to cool slightly. Add the peas and remaining rosemary and place the roasting tin over a hotplate. Cook over medium heat for 5 minutes, or until the peas are cooked. Drain the pasta, divide among four bowls and top with the veal ragout.

nutrition per serve
Fat 5 g; Protein 51.5 g; Carbohydrate 81 g; Dietary Fibre 10 g; Cholesterol 125 mg; 2605 kJ (620 Cal)

shopping tip

Most butchers sell veal shin cut into osso buco pieces. If it is sold in a whole piece, ask the butcher to cut it into 3–4 cm (1¼–1½ inch) thick pieces.

200 rice and red lentil pilau

ingredients

- 1 tablespoon coriander seeds
- 1 tablespoon cardamom seeds
- 1 tablespoon cumin seeds
- 1 teaspoon whole black peppercorns
- 1 teaspoon whole cloves
- 1 small cinnamon stick, roughly crushed
- 1/4 cup (60 ml/2 fl oz) oil
- 1 onion, chopped
- 3 cloves garlic, chopped
- 1 cup (200 g/6 1/2 oz) basmati rice
- 1 cup (250 g/8 oz) red lentils
- 3 cups (750 ml/24 fl oz) hot vegetable stock
- 3 spring onions, thinly sliced

preparation: 15 minutes
cooking: 30 minutes
serves: 4–6

1 To make the garam masala, combine the coriander seeds, cardamom seeds, cumin seeds, peppercorns, cloves and cinnamon stick in a dry frying pan and shake over medium heat for 1 minute, or until aromatic. Transfer to a blender or spice mill and grind to a fine powder.

2 Heat the oil in a large saucepan over medium heat. Add the onion, garlic and 3 teaspoons of the garam masala and cook, stirring, for 3 minutes, or until the onion has softened.

3 Stir in the rice and lentils and cook for a further 2 minutes. Add the stock and stir. Bring slowly to the boil, then reduce the heat and simmer, covered, for 20 minutes, or until the stock is absorbed and the rice is cooked. Fluff with a fork and serve garnished with the spring onion.

nutrition per serve (6)
Fat 10 g; Protein 5.5 g; Carbohydrate 32 g; Dietary Fibre 3 g; Cholesterol 0 g; 1012 kJ (240 Cal)

cooking hint

If you are short of time, you can use a ready-made garam masala spice blend. It is available from delicatessens and some supermarkets. Store leftover spices in an airtight jar.

free-form mushroom lasagne

ingredients

- 10 g (1/4 oz) dried porcini mushrooms
- 350 g (11 oz) assorted mushrooms
- 30 g (1 oz) butter
- 1 small onion, halved and thinly sliced
- 1 tablespoon chopped fresh thyme
- 3 egg yolks
- 1/2 cup (125 ml/4 fl oz) thick cream
- 1 cup (100 g/3 1/2 oz) grated Parmesan
- 8 fresh lasagne sheets (10 x 25 cm/4 x 10 inch)

preparation: 10 minutes + 15 minutes soaking
cooking: 15 minutes
serves: 4

1 Soak the porcini in 1/4 cup (60 ml/2 fl oz) boiling water for 15 minutes. Strain through a sieve, reserving the liquid. Cut the larger mushrooms in half.

2 Heat the butter in a frying pan and cook the onion over medium heat for 1–2 minutes, or until just softened. Add the thyme and mushrooms (including the porcini) and cook for 1–2 minutes, or until softened. Pour in the reserved mushroom liquid and cook for 1–2 minutes, or until the liquid has evaporated.

3 Beat the egg yolks, cream and half the Parmesan in a large bowl. Cook the lasagne sheets in a large saucepan of boiling water for 2–3 minutes, stirring gently. Drain well, then toss the sheets gently through the egg mixture while hot—the heat from the lasagne sheets will cook the egg.

4 Briefly reheat the mushrooms. To serve, place a sheet of folded lasagne on a plate, top with some mushrooms, then another sheet of folded lasagne. Drizzle with any remaining egg mixture and sprinkle with the remaining Parmesan.

nutrition per serve
Fat 30 g; Protein 20 g; Carbohydrate 30 g; Dietary Fibre 4.5 g; Cholesterol 213 mg; 1950 kJ (465 Cal)

cooking hint

Discard any porcini mushrooms that remain woody and tough after soaking. You can use any combination of mushrooms, such as field, Swiss or pine.

spaghetti with herb, garlic and chilli oil

ingredients

- 1 cup (250 ml/8 fl oz) extra virgin olive oil
- 2 fresh bird's eye chillies, seeded and thinly sliced
- 5–6 large cloves garlic, crushed
- 500 g (1 lb) spaghetti
- 100 g (3½ oz) thinly sliced prosciutto
- ½ cup (30 g/1 oz) chopped fresh flat-leaf parsley
- 2 tablespoons chopped fresh basil
- 2 tablespoons chopped fresh oregano
- ¾ cup (75 g/2½ oz) grated Parmesan

preparation: 15 minutes
cooking: 15 minutes
serves: 4–6

1 Pour the oil into a small saucepan with the chilli and garlic. Slowly heat the oil over low heat for about 12 minutes to infuse the oil with the garlic and chilli. Don't allow the oil to reach smoking point or the garlic will burn and taste bitter.

2 Meanwhile, cook the spaghetti in a large saucepan of boiling water according to the packet instructions until *al dente*. Drain well and return to the pan. Lay the prosciutto on a grill tray and cook under a hot grill for 2 minutes each side, or until crispy. Cool and break into pieces.

3 Pour the hot oil mixture over the spaghetti and toss well with the prosciutto, herbs and Parmesan. Season to taste, then serve.

nutrition per serve (6)
Fat 44 g; Protein 17.5 g; Carbohydrate 59.5 g; Dietary Fibre 5.5 g; Cholesterol 20.5 mg; 2945 kJ (705 Cal)

variation

You can use bacon instead of the prosciutto, but it will need to be cooked for a little longer on each side to become crisp.

madras lamb pilau

ingredients

- 1/4 cup (60 ml/2 fl oz) oil
- 2 onions, thinly sliced
- 1 cup (250 g/8 oz) plain yoghurt
- 1/4 cup (60 g/2 oz) Madras curry paste
- 2 cups (400 g/13 oz) basmati rice, rinsed well
- 8 large lamb cutlets, trimmed
- 4 tablespoons chopped fresh mint
- 1/2 cup (60 g/2 oz) slivered almonds, lightly toasted

preparation: 20 minutes
cooking: 35 minutes
serves: 4

1 Heat 2 tablespoons of the oil in a large saucepan, add the onion and cook over medium heat for about 5 minutes, or until soft. Remove half with a slotted spoon and keep warm. Add 200 g (6½ oz) yoghurt and 2 tablespoons curry paste to the pan. Cook, stirring, for 2 minutes. Stir in the rice until well coated. Pour in 2 cups (500 ml/16 fl oz) water and bring to the boil, then reduce the heat to medium–low and cook for about 20 minutes, or until the water is absorbed and the rice is tender.

2 Meanwhile, smear the cutlets with the remaining curry paste and marinate for 5 minutes. Heat the remaining oil in a frying pan over high heat, then cook the cutlets for 3–4 minutes on each side, or until cooked to your liking. Remove from the heat, cover with foil and rest. Combine the remaining yoghurt with 1 tablespoon of the mint.

3 To serve, stir the remaining mint through the rice, season, then divide among four plates. Top with the remaining onions, the lamb and almonds. Serve with a dollop of the minted yoghurt on the side.

nutrition per serve
Fat 39 g; Protein 46 g; Carbohydrate 87.5 g; Dietary Fibre 4.5 g; Cholesterol 110 mg; 3720 kJ (890 Cal)

cooking hint

Greek yoghurt is ideal for this recipe because it gives a thick and creamy texture.

sweet potato and sage risotto

ingredients

- 1.25 litres chicken stock
- 8 slices prosciutto
- 100 ml (3½ fl oz) extra virgin olive oil
- 1 red onion, cut into wedges
- 600 g (1¼ lb) orange sweet potato, peeled and cut into 2.5 cm (1 inch) cubes
- 2 cups (440 g/14 oz) arborio rice
- ¾ cup (75 g/2½ oz) grated Parmesan
- 3 tablespoons chopped fresh sage

preparation: 15 minutes
cooking: 35 minutes
serves: 4

1 Bring the stock to the boil in a saucepan, then reduce the heat, cover, and keep at a low simmer. Grill the prosciutto under a hot grill for 1–2 minutes on each side, or until crispy.

2 Heat ¼ cup (60 ml/2 fl oz) oil in a large saucepan, add the onion and cook over medium heat for 2–3 minutes, or until softened. Add the sweet potato and rice, and stir through until well coated in the oil.

3 Add ½ cup (125 ml/4 fl oz) hot stock, stirring constantly over medium heat until it is absorbed. Continue adding more stock, ½ cup (125 ml/4 fl oz) at a time, stirring constantly for 20–25 minutes, or until all the stock is absorbed, and the rice is tender and creamy in texture. Stir in the Parmesan and 2 tablespoons of the sage. Season.

4 Spoon into four bowls and drizzle with the remaining oil. Break the prosciutto into pieces and sprinkle over the risotto, then garnish with the remaining sage. Serve immediately.

nutrition per serve
Fat 30 g; Protein 18 g; Carbohydrate 110 g; Dietary Fibre 5.5 g; Cholesterol 18 mg; 3302 kJ (790 Cal)

cooking hint

When cooked, arborio rice should be soft but with a tiny 'nuttiness' or white speck in the centre of each grain. Each grain of rice should be separate but creamy.

tagliatelle with salmon and creamy dill dressing

ingredients

- 350 g (11 oz) fresh tagliatelle
- 1/4 cup (60 ml/2 fl oz) olive oil
- 3 × 200 g (6 1/2 oz) salmon fillets, skinned and boned
- 3 cloves garlic, crushed
- 1 1/2 cups (375 ml/12 fl oz) cream
- 1 1/2 tablespoons chopped fresh dill
- 1 teaspoon mustard powder
- 1 tablespoon lemon juice
- 40 g (1 1/4 oz) shaved Parmesan

preparation: 10 minutes
cooking: 15 minutes
serves: 4

1 Cook the tagliatelle in a large saucepan of boiling water according to the packet instructions until *al dente*. Drain well, then toss with 1 tablespoon of the olive oil.

2 Meanwhile, heat the remaining oil in a large, deep frying pan and cook the salmon for 2 minutes on each side, or until crisp on the outside but still pink inside. Remove from the pan, cut into 2 cm (3/4 inch) cubes, and keep warm.

3 In the same pan add the garlic and cook for 30 seconds, or until fragrant. Add the cream, dill and mustard powder, bring to the boil, then reduce the heat and simmer, stirring, for 4–5 minutes, or until thickened. Season to taste with salt and freshly ground black pepper.

4 Add the salmon and any juices plus the lemon juice to the creamy dill sauce and stir until warmed through. Gently toss the sauce and salmon through the pasta and divide among four serving bowls. Sprinkle with Parmesan and serve.

nutrition per serve
Fat 66 g; Protein 45 g; Carbohydrate 51 g; Dietary Fibre 1.5 g; Cholesterol 215 mg; 4100 kJ (980 Cal)

shopping tip

Ask your fishmonger to skin and bone your salmon fillet. If you prefer, use 2 teaspoons Dijon mustard instead of the mustard powder.

AL DENTE PASTA

Prepare all the ingredients for a pasta sauce from the adjacent recipes so that they can be cooked while the pasta is boiling.

Bring a large saucepan of water to the boil, add a pinch of salt, then add the pasta and cook according to the packet instructions, until *al dente*. Meanwhile, cook your sauce. Drain the pasta. If the pasta will be sitting around for a little while before being added to the sauce, return it to the pan and toss through a little olive oil to prevent it from sticking together.

serves 4

fresh tomato and basil sauce

Heat 1/3 cup (80 ml/2 3/4 fl oz) extra virgin olive oil in a frying pan and cook 5 cloves of thinly sliced garlic over low heat for 1 minute. As soon as the garlic begins to change colour, remove the pan from the heat and add another tablespoon of oil. Add the cooked pasta to the pan with 6 seeded and chopped vine-ripened tomatoes and 3/4 cup (25 g/3/4 oz) torn fresh basil. Season generously with salt and freshly ground black pepper. Toss well and serve drizzled with a little extra virgin olive oil and sprinkled with a generous amount of good-quality coarsely grated Parmesan.

TO SERVE: 400 g (13 oz) spaghetti is ideal with this sauce.

zucchini and ricotta sauce

Heat 1/4 cup (60 ml/2 fl oz) olive oil in a frying pan and cook 750 g (1 1/2 lb) thinly sliced small zucchini in two batches over high heat, tossing frequently for 5–6 minutes or until softened and golden brown. Return all the zucchini to the pan, then add 3 cloves crushed garlic. Toss for 2–3 minutes, or until the garlic is lightly browned. Add the pasta and 350 g (11 oz) drained, crumbled ricotta, 3/4 cup (25 g/3/4 oz) torn fresh basil and 80 g (2 3/4 oz) coarsely grated Parmesan. Season to taste. Toss well, drizzle with a little extra virgin olive oil and sprinkle with extra grated Parmesan

TO SERVE: 500 g (1 lb) spirali or gemelli is ideal for this sauce.

anchovy, garlic and chilli sauce

Heat ½ cup (125 ml/4 fl oz) extra virgin olive oil in a frying pan and cook 4 cloves crushed garlic over low heat until just beginning to turn golden. Add 10 chopped anchovy fillets and 1 teaspoon crushed chilli flakes and cook for a further minute. Add the cooked, drained pasta to the frying pan with 2 tablespoons lemon juice, 2 teaspoons grated lemon rind and 3 tablespoons each of chopped fresh parsley, basil and mint. Season to taste, add ½ cup (45 g/ 1½ oz) coarsely grated Parmesan and toss well. Serve drizzled with a little extra virgin olive oil and a generous amount of extra shaved Parmesan.

TO SERVE: 400 g (13 oz) spaghettini is ideal for this sauce.

creamy tuna, tomato and oregano sauce

Heat 2 tablespoons olive oil in a saucepan and cook 2 cloves finely chopped garlic over medium heat until just beginning to turn brown. Add 2 teaspoons dried oregano and two 400 g (13 oz) cans chopped tomatoes. Season lightly add simmer for 12–15 minutes, or until the sauce has thickened and reduced. Add 1½ cups (375 ml/ 12 fl oz) cream and simmer for 3–4 minutes. Add a 300 g (10 oz) can of drained tuna, 2 teaspoons grated lemon rind and stir gently to combine. Season to taste. Add the pasta, stir well and serve. You may wish to garnish with a little grated Parmesan.

TO SERVE: 500 g (1 lb) penne is ideal for this sauce.

cooking hint

To peel tomatoes, score a cross in the base of the tomatoes. Place them in a bowl of boiling water for 30 seconds, then plunge into cold water and peel the skin away from the cross.

From left to right: Fresh tomato and basil sauce, Zucchini and ricotta sauce, Anchovy, garlic and chilli sauce, Creamy tuna, tomato and oregano sauce.

chicken, mushroom and almond pilau

ingredients

- 1½ cups (300 g/10 oz) basmati rice
- 2 tablespoons oil
- 1 large onion, chopped
- 3–4 cloves garlic, crushed
- 1 tablespoon finely chopped fresh ginger
- 500 g (1 lb) chicken tenderloin fillets, trimmed and cut into pieces
- 300 g (10 oz) Swiss brown mushrooms, sliced
- ¾ cup (90 g/3 oz) slivered almonds, toasted
- 1½–2 teaspoons garam masala, dry-roasted
- ½ cup (125 g/4 oz) plain yoghurt
- 1 tablespoon finely chopped fresh coriander leaves, plus extra leaves, to garnish

preparation: 15 minutes
cooking: 35 minutes
serves: 4

1 Rinse the rice under cold water until the water runs clear. Drain. Heat the oil in a large saucepan and stir in the onion, garlic and ginger. Reduce the heat to medium and cook, covered, for 5 minutes, or until the onion is browned. Increase the heat to high, add the chicken and cook, stirring, for 3–4 minutes, or until the chicken is lightly browned.

2 Stir in the mushrooms, almonds and garam masala. Cook, covered, for a further 3 minutes, or until the mushrooms are soft. Remove the lid and cook, stirring, for 2 minutes, or until the liquid has completely evaporated. Remove the chicken from the pan.

3 Add the rice to the pan and stir for 30 seconds, or until well coated in the mushroom and onion mixture. Add 1½ cups (375 ml/12 fl oz) water and bring to the boil, stirring frequently, for 2 minutes, or until most of the water has evaporated. Return the chicken to the pan. Cover, reduce the heat to low and steam for 15 minutes, or until the rice is cooked.

4 Meanwhile, place the yoghurt and chopped coriander in a small bowl and mix together.

5 Fluff the rice with a fork, then divide among serving bowls and top with a dollop of the yoghurt mixture. Garnish with coriander leaves, then serve.

nutrition per serve
Fat 31.5 g; Protein 38 g; Carbohydrate 67 g; Dietary Fibre 6 g; Cholesterol 112.5 mg; 2933 kJ (698 Cal)

cooking hint

The rice needs to be rinsed really well to remove the excess starch and to make the pilaf light and fluffy.

baked macaroni with tomato sauce

ingredients

200 g (6½ oz) macaroni
160 g (5½ oz) butter
¼ cup (30 g/1 oz) plain flour
2½ cups (625 ml/20 fl oz) milk
1 egg, lightly beaten
1½ cups (185 g/6 oz) grated Cheddar
2 cloves garlic, crushed
2 ripe tomatoes, seeded and diced

preparation: 15 minutes + 5 minutes resting
cooking: 35 minutes
serves: 4

1 Preheat the oven to moderate 180°C (350°F/Gas 4). Lightly grease four shallow 1 cup (250 ml/8 fl oz) ovenproof dishes or ramekins. Bring a large saucepan of lightly salted water to the boil and cook the macaroni according to the packet instructions until *al dente*. Drain well.

2 Meanwhile, melt 60 g (2 oz) of the butter in a large saucepan, add the flour and cook, stirring, over low heat for 1 minute. Remove from the heat and gradually add the milk, stirring until smooth. Return to the heat and cook, stirring, over medium heat for 4 minutes, or until the mixture boils and thickens. Reduce the heat and simmer for 1 minute. Remove from the heat and season.

3 Add the pasta, egg and two-thirds of the cheese, and stir until well combined. Spoon into the dishes and sprinkle with the remaining cheese. Place the dishes in a roasting tin and fill with boiling water until it comes halfway up the sides of the dishes. Bake for 25 minutes, or until set. Remove from the dish and leave to rest for 5 minutes.

4 Meanwhile, to make the sauce, melt the remaining butter in a frying pan. Add the garlic and tomato, and stir over medium heat for 2 minutes. Turn the moulds out onto four serving plates and spoon the warm sauce around the outside. Garnish with some fresh herbs, if desired. Serve immediately.

nutrition per serve
Fat 57 g; Protein 26 g; Carbohydrate 50 g; Dietary Fibre 4 g; Cholesterol 215 mg; 3385 kJ (810 Cal)

variation

You can use many other cheeses or a combination of your favourite cheeses in the sauce. Try using Gruyère, blue vein, feta, goat's cheese or Parmesan.

pasta pronto

ingredients

2 tablespoons extra virgin olive oil
4 cloves garlic, finely chopped
1 small fresh red chilli, finely chopped
3 x 400 g (13 oz) cans chopped tomatoes
1 teaspoon sugar
1/3 cup (80 ml/2 3/4 fl oz) dry white wine
3 tablespoons chopped fresh herbs
400 g (13 oz) vermicelli
30 g (1 oz) shaved Parmesan

preparation: 10 minutes
cooking: 15 minutes
serves: 4

1 Heat the oil in a large deep frying pan, add the garlic and chilli and cook, stirring, for 1 minute. Add the chopped tomatoes, sugar, wine, herbs and 1 3/4 cups (440 ml/14 fl oz) water. Bring to the boil over high heat and season with salt and freshly ground black pepper.

2 Reduce the heat to medium and add the pasta, breaking the strands if they are too long to fit into the pan. Cook for 10 minutes, or until the pasta is cooked, stirring often to stop the pasta strands from sticking together. The pasta will thicken the sauce as it cooks. Season to taste. Divide among four serving bowls and sprinkle with shaved Parmesan.

nutrition per serve
Fat 13.5 g; Protein 17 g; Carbohydrate 81.5 g; Dietary Fibre 9.5 g; Cholesterol 7 mg; 2225 kJ (530 Cal)

variation

You can vary this meal by changing the herbs that you use; we have used basil and parsley, but you can try oregano, thyme, marjoram or rosemary.
If you don't have vermicelli, use spaghettini or angel hair pasta instead.

ingredients

400 g (13 oz) spaghetti
1/3 cup (80 ml/2 3/4 fl oz) extra virgin olive oil
200 g (6 1/2 oz) fresh asparagus
1 cup (155 g/5 oz) frozen peas
1 cup (155 g/5 oz) frozen broad beans
1 leek, thinly sliced
2 tablespoons finely chopped fresh flat-leaf parsley
1 cup (250 ml/8 fl oz) thick cream
1/3 cup (35 g/1 1/4 oz) grated Parmesan

preparation: 15 minutes
cooking: 15 minutes
serves: 4

1 Bring a large saucepan of water to the boil, add the spaghetti and cook according to the packet instructions until *al dente*. Rinse and drain well, then return to the pan, toss with 2 tablespoons of the oil and keep warm.

2 Meanwhile, trim the asparagus and cut into 5 cm (2 inch) lengths. Bring a saucepan of water to the boil and cook the asparagus and peas for 2 minutes, or until bright green and tender. Remove with a slotted spoon and plunge into cold water. Return the saucepan to the boil and cook the broad beans for 2 minutes, or until tender. Drain, cool a little, then slip off their skins.

3 Heat the remaining oil in a frying pan and cook the leek over low heat for 2–3 minutes, or until soft but not brown. Add the blanched vegetables and cook for 1 minute, or until warmed through. Stir in the parsley and cream and simmer for 2–3 minutes. Toss the sauce and Parmesan through the pasta, season well with salt and freshly ground black pepper, then serve.

nutrition per serve
Fat 43 g; Protein 21 g; Carbohydrate 77 g; Dietary Fibre 10.5 g; Cholesterol 73 mg; 3270 kJ (780 Cal)

variation

When fresh broad beans and peas are in season, you can use them instead of the frozen ones. Allow yourself a little extra preparation time to peel the pods before cooking.

quick mushroom and ricotta cannelloni

ingredients

- 500 g (1 lb) button mushrooms
- 200 g (6½ oz) fresh lasagne sheets
- 2 tablespoons olive oil
- 3 cloves garlic, crushed
- 2 tablespoons lemon juice
- 400 g (13 oz) ricotta
- 3 tablespoons torn fresh basil
- 425 g (14 oz) bottled tomato pasta sauce
- 1 cup (150 g/5 oz) grated mozzarella

preparation: 15 minutes
cooking: 30 minutes
serves: 4

1 Preheat the oven to moderate 180°C (350°F/Gas 4). Place the mushrooms in a food processor and pulse until finely chopped.

2 Cut the lasagne sheets into twelve 13 x 16 cm (4¼ x 6½ inch) rectangles.

3 Heat the oil in a large frying pan over medium heat. Add the garlic and chopped mushrooms and cook, stirring, for 3 minutes. Add the lemon juice and cook for a further 2 minutes, or until softened. Transfer the mushroom mixture to a sieve over a bowl to collect the juices, pressing with a spoon to remove as much moisture as possible. Reserve the liquid and transfer the mushroom to a bowl with the ricotta and basil. Season well with plenty of salt and freshly ground black pepper and mix well.

4 Lay one of the pasta sheets on a work surface and place heaped tablespoons of the mixture along one long edge. Roll up and place in a greased ovenproof ceramic dish that is large enough to fit all the cannelloni in a single layer. Repeat with the remaining mixture and lasagne sheets.

5 Pour the reserved mushroom cooking liquid over the cannelloni, then pour on the pasta sauce. Sprinkle with cheese and bake for 25 minutes, or until golden and bubbling. Serve with salad.

nutrition per serve
Fat 29.5 g; Protein 33 g; Carbohydrate 37.5 g; Dietary Fibre 6 g; Cholesterol 90 mg; 2290 kJ (545 Cal)

variation

Instead of fresh lasagne sheets you can use dried cannelloni shells readily available at supermarkets. Fill the tubes with the mixture and cook according to the recipe.

agnolotti with salmon, capers and brown butter

ingredients

- ½ cup (125 ml/4 fl oz) olive oil
- 100 g (3½ oz) capers, drained and patted dry
- 500 g (1 lb) salmon fillets, skin removed
- 625 g (1 lb 5 oz) ricotta agnolotti
- 150 g (5 oz) butter
- 1½ teaspoons finely grated lemon rind
- 2 tablespoons lemon juice
- 3 tablespoons roughly chopped fresh flat-leaf parsley

preparation: 10 minutes
cooking: 15 minutes
serves: 4

1 Heat half the oil in a small frying pan and cook the capers over high heat for 3–4 minutes, or until golden and crispy. Remove from the oil and drain on crumpled paper towels.

2 Season the salmon fillets on both sides with salt and pepper. Heat the remaining oil in a non-stick frying pan and cook the salmon for 2–3 minutes on each side, or until just cooked through but still pink in the centre. Remove from the pan and keep warm. Gently break the salmon into flakes with your fingers, being careful to remove any bones.

3 Cook the agnolotti in a large saucepan of rapidly boiling water, according to the packet instructions, until *al dente*. Drain, return to the pan and keep warm.

4 Heat the butter in a frying pan over low heat for 5 minutes, or until golden. Quickly add the lemon rind, lemon juice and parsley. Divide the pasta among serving dishes, top with the flaked salmon and pour on the brown butter. Scatter with the capers and serve immediately.

nutrition per serve
Fat 68 g; Protein 35.5 g; Carbohydrate 43.5 g; Dietary Fibre 5 g; Cholesterol 181 mg; 3865 kJ (925 Cal)

cooking hint

It is important to cook the butter enough that it has a 'nutty' flavour, but not too much that it burns and becomes bitter. The lemon juice stops the butter cooking further, so add it as soon as the butter is ready.
Agnolotti is interchangeable with ravioli or tortellini.

ham tortellini with nutty herb sauce

ingredients

- 500 g (1 lb) ham and cheese tortellini
- 60 g (2 oz) butter
- 1 cup (100 g/3½ oz) walnuts, chopped
- ⅔ cup (100 g/3½ oz) pine nuts
- 2 tablespoons finely chopped fresh flat-leaf parsley
- 2 teaspoons chopped fresh thyme
- ¼ cup (60 g/2 oz) ricotta
- ¼ cup (60 ml/2 fl oz) thick cream

preparation: 15 minutes
cooking: 10 minutes
serves: 4–6

1 Bring a large saucepan of water to the boil, add the tortellini and cook according to the packet instructions until *al dente*. Drain and return to the pan.

2 Meanwhile, heat the butter in a frying pan over medium heat until foaming. Add the walnuts and pine nuts and stir for 5 minutes, or until golden brown. Add the parsley and thyme and season to taste with salt and freshly ground black pepper.

3 Beat the ricotta and cream together. Add the nutty sauce to the pasta and toss. Divide among serving bowls and top with the ricotta cream.

nutrition per serve (6)
Fat 47 g; Protein 21.5 g; Carbohydrate 23 g; Dietary Fibre 3.5 g; Cholesterol 84.5 mg; 2495 kJ (595 Cal)

variation

Add 150 g (5 oz) drained and thinly sliced marinated sun-dried tomatoes to the pan when adding the herbs.

angel hair pasta with creamy garlic prawns

ingredients

- 2 tablespoons olive oil
- 16 raw medium prawns, peeled
- 1 leek, chopped
- 6 cloves garlic, crushed
- 1/2 teaspoon chilli flakes
- 1/2 cup (125 ml/4 fl oz) dry white wine
- 200 ml (6 1/2 fl oz) cream
- 250 g (8 oz) angel hair pasta
- 3 tablespoons chopped fresh flat-leaf parsley

preparation: 15 minutes
cooking: 15 minutes
serves: 4

1 Heat 1 tablespoon of the oil in a frying pan, season the prawns with salt and pepper, add to the pan and cook over high heat for 2–3 minutes, or until the prawns are cooked and pink. Remove from the pan, cover and keep warm.

2 Heat the remaining oil in the same pan, add the leek and cook, stirring, over medium heat for 2–3 minutes, or until softened. Add the garlic and chilli flakes and stir for 1 minute. Pour in the wine, reduce the heat and simmer for 4 minutes, or until reduced. Add the cream and simmer for 3 minutes, or until just thickened.

3 Meanwhile, cook the angel hair pasta in a large saucepan of boiling water according to the packet instructions until *al dente*. Drain and return to the pan.

4 Stir the parsley into the sauce and season well with salt and freshly ground black pepper. Add to the pasta and stir to coat. Divide among the serving bowls and top with four prawns per bowl.

nutrition per serve
Fat 32 g; Protein 19.5 g; Carbohydrate 43.5 g; Dietary Fibre 4.5 g; Cholesterol 142.5 mg; 2420 kJ (580 Cal)

serving tip

The prawns will look very pretty if their tails are left intact when you peel them. Provide a plate on the table for the discarded tails.

spicy sausage pilau

ingredients

30 g (1 oz) butter
1 large onion, thinly sliced
2 cloves garlic, crushed
300 g (10 oz) chorizo sausage, thinly sliced
2 cups (400 g/13 oz) long-grain rice
1 bay leaf
1 litre chicken stock
1 cup (155 g/5 oz) frozen peas
1/2 cup (80 g/2 3/4 oz) sun-dried capsicum in oil, drained and thinly sliced
4 spring onions, thinly sliced
shaved Parmesan, to serve

preparation: 20 minutes
cooking: 40 minutes
serves: 4–6

1 Melt the butter in a large saucepan over medium heat. Add the onion and garlic and cook, stirring, for 5 minutes, or until the onion is soft. Add the chorizo and cook, stirring, for 2 minutes. Add the rice and bay leaf and stir for 1 minute, or until the rice is well coated in the mixture.

2 Pour in the stock and bring to the boil. Continue boiling until tunnels appear in the rice, stir quickly, then cover and reduce the heat to low. Cook for 20 minutes, without stirring.

3 Sprinkle the peas and capsicum strips over the rice. Cover, remove from the heat and leave for 10 minutes. Sprinkle with the spring onion, then fluff with a fork. Sprinkle with Parmesan, then serve.

nutrition per serve (6)
Fat 21 g; Protein 13 g; Carbohydrate 58 g; Dietary Fibre 5 g; Cholesterol 40 g; 1987 kJ (475 Cal)

shopping tip

If you can't find chorizo, substitute any spicy smoked pork sausage.
Sun-dried capsicum can be used instead of the tomatoes, or you can use a combination of both.

farfalle with spinach and bacon

ingredients

- 400 g (13 oz) farfalle
- 2 tablespoons extra virgin olive oil
- 250 g (8 oz) bacon, chopped
- 1 red onion, finely chopped
- 250 g (8 oz) baby English spinach leaves, stems trimmed
- 35 g (1¼ oz) crumbled goat's feta

preparation: 10 minutes
cooking: 15 minutes
serves: 4

1 Cook the pasta in a large saucepan of boiling water according to the packet instructions until *al dente*. Drain and return to the pan.

2 Meanwhile, heat the oil in a frying pan, add the bacon and cook over medium heat for 3 minutes, or until golden. Add the onion and cook for a further 4 minutes, or until softened. Toss the spinach leaves through the onion and bacon mixture for 30 seconds, or until the leaves are just wilted.

3 Add the bacon and spinach mixture to the pasta. Season with salt and black pepper and toss well. Spoon into four warm bowls and scatter with the crumbled feta. Serve immediately.

nutrition per serve
Fat 19 g; Protein 28 g; Carbohydrate 73 g; Dietary Fibre 7 g; Cholesterol 42 mg; 2415 kJ (575 Cal)

variation

Stir through ½ cup chopped mixed fresh herbs (e.g. basil, parsley or mint) just before serving.
Farfalle is sometimes referred to as the 'bow-tie' pasta because of its resemblance to the shape of a bow-tie.

spanish saffron chicken and rice

ingredients

- 1/4 cup (60 ml/2 fl oz) olive oil
- 4 chicken thighs and 6 drumsticks
- 1 large red onion, finely chopped
- 1 large green capsicum, two-thirds diced and one-third julienned
- 3 teaspoons sweet paprika
- 400 g (13 oz) can diced tomatoes
- 1 1/4 cups (275 g/9 oz) arborio rice
- 1/2 teaspoon ground saffron

preparation: 15 minutes
cooking: 1 hour
serves: 4

1 Heat 2 tablespoons of the oil in a large, deep frying pan over high heat. Season the chicken pieces with salt and pepper, add them to the pan in batches and cook until browned. Remove from the pan, then discard any excess fat from the base of the pan.

2 Reduce the heat to medium and add the remaining oil. Add the onion and diced capsicum and cook gently for 5 minutes. Stir in the paprika and cook for 30 seconds. Add the tomato and simmer for 1–3 minutes, or until the sauce thickens.

3 Pour 3 1/2 cups (875 ml/28 fl oz) boiling water into the pan, stir well, then add the rice and saffron. Return the chicken to the pan and stir to combine. Season with salt and pepper. Bring to the boil, then reduce the heat to medium–low, cover with a lid and simmer for 20–30 minutes, or until all the liquid has been absorbed and the chicken is tender. Stir in the julienned capsicum, then cover and allow to stand for a few minutes before serving

nutrition per serve
Fat 79 g; Protein 94.5 g; Carbohydrate 56.5 g; Dietary Fibre 2.5 g; Cholesterol 511 mg; 5490 kJ (1310 Cal)

variation

Add 1 thinly sliced chorizo sausage to the pan after you have removed the chicken. Cook for 1–2 minutes or until lightly browned, then remove. Return to the pan when you add the chicken.

fried rice with chinese barbecued pork

ingredients

- 6 spring onions
- 150 g (5 oz) snow peas
- 200 g (6½ oz) Chinese barbecued pork
- 3 teaspoons sesame oil
- 2 eggs, lightly beaten
- 2 cloves garlic, finely chopped
- 3 cups (555 g/1 lb 2 oz) cold cooked white long-grain rice
- 2 tablespoons soy sauce

preparation: 15 minutes
cooking: 10 minutes
serves: 4

1 Cut the spring onions and snow peas into very thin shreds on the diagonal. Cut the barbecued pork into thin slices.

2 Heat a wok until hot, add 1 teaspoon of the oil and swirl to coat the side. Add the egg and swirl over the base until just set. Turn over and cook until just lightly browned, then remove from the wok. Allow the egg to cool slightly, then roll up and cut into 1 cm (½ inch) thick slices.

3 While the wok is still very hot, add the remaining oil, then the garlic, spring onion and snow peas and stir-fry until slightly soft. Add the pork, rice, soy sauce and strips of omelette and toss until heated through and thoroughly combined—the soy sauce should turn the rice brown. Remove from the heat and serve immediately.

nutrition per serve
Fat 10 g; Protein 22.5 g; Carbohydrate 42 g; Dietary Fibre 2.5 g; Cholesterol 147 mg; 1460 kJ (350 Cal)

cooking hint

You will need to cook about 1 cup (200 g/61/2 oz) rice to yield 3 cups cooked rice.

salads & sides

224 mixed steamed asian greens

ingredients

1 lime, thinly sliced
1 tablespoon chopped fresh ginger
500 g (1 lb) mixed Asian greens, trimmed (e.g. bok choy, choy sum, snake beans or Chinese broccoli)
1/2 teaspoon sesame oil
2 teaspoons toasted sesame seeds

preparation: 10 minutes
cooking: 5 minutes
serves: 4–6

1 Place the lime, ginger and 3 cups (750 ml/24 fl oz) water in a wok or large saucepan and bring to the boil. Line a bamboo steamer with bamboo paper and place it over the wok or saucepan. Add the mixed Asian greens to the steamer and steam for 2–3 minutes, or until tender.

2 Toss the sesame oil through the vegetables. Transfer to a serving plate, sprinkle with toasted sesame seeds and serve.

nutrition per serve (6)
Fat 1 g; Protein 1 g; Carbohydrate 1 g; Dietary Fibre 1.5 g; Cholesterol 0 mg; 75 kJ (20 Cal)

variation

Drizzle the steamed greens with a little oyster sauce or kecap manis instead of the sesame oil and sesame seeds. Alternatively, lightly cook 2 cloves crushed garlic in 1 tablespoon oil, add the sesame oil and toss with the greens in the pan.

kipfler potato salad

ingredients

- 1 kg (2 lb) kipfler potatoes or other waxy potatoes, washed
- 125 g (4 oz) bacon, chopped
- 2 teaspoons olive oil
- 2 spring onions, chopped
- ½ cup (125 g/4 oz) sour cream
- 2 tablespoons olive oil
- 2 tablespoons red wine vinegar
- 2 teaspoons Dijon mustard
- 2 teaspoons wholegrain mustard

preparation: 15 minutes
cooking: 25 minutes
serves: 6

1 Cook the potatoes in a large saucepan of boiling water for 20 minutes, or until tender. Drain, allow to cool slightly, then cut into 3 cm (1¼ inch) slices on the diagonal. Transfer to a large serving bowl.

2 Heat the oil in a frying pan over medium heat, add the bacon and cook for about 5 minutes, or until crispy and golden. Add to the potato along with the spring onions.

3 To make the dressing, put the sour cream, olive oil, red wine vinegar and both types of mustard in a small bowl and mix together thoroughly. Spoon into the bowl with the potatoes and gently toss to combine. Season with a little salt and freshly ground black pepper and serve.

nutrition per serve
Fat 19.5 g; Protein 8.5g; Carbohydrate 23 g; Dietary Fibre 3.5 g; Cholesterol 39 mg; 1270 kJ (305 Cal)

variation

Add 1–2 tablespoons of chopped fresh dill instead of the spring onion.
For those who are watching their weight, this salad is also delicious without the sour cream. Toss the warm potatoes with the bacon, spring onion, oil, vinegar and mustard and serve warm.

226 feta, beetroot and rocket salad

ingredients

2 x 340 g (11 oz) jars baby beetroots, drained and cut into quarters
200 g (6½ oz) baby rocket leaves
300 g (10 oz) marinated feta, drained and cut into even-sized cubes
¼ cup (60 ml/2 fl oz) olive oil
1 tablespoon balsamic vinegar

preparation: 5 minutes
cooking: nil
serves: 6

1 Place the beetroot, rocket and feta in a large serving bowl and mix together thoroughly.

2 To make the dressing, place the oil and balsamic vinegar in a small bowl and whisk together, then pour over the salad and toss well. Season with freshly ground black pepper and serve.

nutrition per serve
Fat 21.5 g; Protein 11 g; Carbohydrate 8 g; Dietary Fibre 2.5 g; Cholesterol 34.5 mg; 1110 kJ (265 Cal)

variation

For a bit of crunch, add 150 g (5 oz) toasted walnuts or pine nuts to the salad. If you are watching your weight, use a low-fat feta.

roasted tomatoes with balsamic and basil

ingredients

- 6 Roma tomatoes, cut in half lengthways
- 1/4 cup (60 ml/2 fl oz) olive oil
- 2 tablespoons balsamic vinegar
- 5 cloves garlic, peeled
- 1 1/2 teaspoons sugar
- small fresh basil leaves, to garnish

preparation: 5 minutes
cooking: 40 minutes
serves: 4–6

1 Preheat the oven to warm 170°C (325°F/Gas 3). Place the tomatoes on a lightly greased baking tray, skin-side-down. Mix the oil with the balsamic vinegar and drizzle over the tomato halves. Bruise the garlic cloves with the back of a knife and scatter over the baking tray between the tomatoes.

2 Sprinkle the sugar over the tomatoes, then cook in the oven for 35–40 minutes, or until quite soft. Arrange the tomatoes on a serving plate, scatter with the roasted garlic and top each tomato half with a small basil leaf. Drizzle with any remaining pan juices and season with salt and freshly ground black pepper.

nutrition per serve (6)
Fat 8.5 g; Protein 1 g; Carbohydrate 2.5 g; Dietary Fibre 1 g; Cholesterol 0 mg; 375 kJ (90 Cal)

cooking hint

If you can't find Roma tomatoes, use round vine-ripened tomatoes instead. Cut them into smaller pieces after roasting.

228 bean salad

ingredients

- 250 g (8 oz) green beans
- 250 g (8 oz) yellow beans
- 1/4 cup (60 ml/2 fl oz) olive oil
- 1 tablespoon lemon juice
- 1 clove garlic, crushed
- 50 g (1 3/4 oz) shaved Parmesan

preparation: 10 minutes
cooking: 5 minutes
serves: 6

1 Bring a saucepan of lightly salted water to the boil. Add the beans and cook for 2 minutes, or until just tender. Drain, plunge into cold water and drain again.

2 Place the oil, lemon juice and garlic in a bowl, season with salt and freshly ground black pepper, and mix together well. Place the beans in a serving bowl, pour on the dressing and toss to coat. Top with shaved Parmesan and serve.

nutrition per serve
Fat 11.5 g; Protein 5 g; Carbohydrate 2 g; Dietary Fibre 2.5 g; Cholesterol 8 mg; 550 kJ (130 Cal)

cooking hint

The smaller the beans, the more tender they will be. For beans to retain their colour they should be cooked in plenty of boiling, salted water.

citrus-glazed carrots

ingredients

- 1 kg (2 lb) baby carrots
- 20 g (3/4 oz) butter
- 2 teaspoons honey
- 1 tablespoon freshly squeezed orange juice
- 2 teaspoons grated orange rind
- chopped fresh flat-leaf parsley, to garnish

preparation: 10 minutes
cooking: 5 minutes
serves: 4–6

1 Trim the leafy tops from the carrots, leaving a small amount of stem intact.

2 Put the butter in a small saucepan over medium heat until melted, then add the honey, orange juice, orange rind and the carrots, and toss until they are all coated in the butter. Cook, covered, over medium heat for 4–5 minutes, or until the carrots are tender. Transfer to a serving plate and sprinkle with chopped fresh flat-leaf parsley. Season with salt and freshly ground black pepper and serve immediately.

nutrition per serve (6)
Fat 3 g; Protein 1 g; Carbohydrate 9.5 g; Dietary Fibre 4 g; Cholesterol 8.5 mg; 280 kJ (65 Cal)

cooking hint

If you can't find baby carrots, use medium ones and cut them into quarters lengthways. These are delicious served with a simple pan-fried chicken breast or steak with a creamy mash or green salad.

238 sugar snap peas with toasted almonds and pancetta

ingredients

- 1/3 cup (40 g/1 1/4 oz) slivered almonds
- 2 teaspoons olive oil
- 1 small onion, chopped
- 2 slices pancetta, finely chopped
- 300 g (10 oz) sugar snap peas

preparation: 10 minutes
cooking: 15 minutes
serves: 4–6

1 Preheat the oven to warm 170°C (325°/Gas 3). Spread the almonds out on a baking tray and cook for 8–10 minutes, or until they are lightly golden.

2 Heat the oil in a large frying pan, add the onion and pancetta and cook over medium heat for 2 minutes. Add the peas and stir-fry for 2–3 minutes, or until tender.

3 Remove from the heat, add the toasted almonds and toss to coat. Transfer the mixture to a serving plate, season with salt and freshly ground black pepper and serve immediately.

nutrition per serve (6)
Fat 5.5 g; Protein 3.5 g; Carbohydrate 3 g; Dietary Fibre 2 g; Cholesterol 1.5 mg; 310 kJ (75 Cal)

variation

You can use bacon instead of the pancetta, and any kind of toasted nuts, such as hazelnuts, pine nuts or walnuts, instead of the almonds.

mini cornbreads

ingredients

1 cup (125 g/4 oz) self-raising flour
1 cup (150 g/5 oz) fine polenta
1 cup (250 ml/8 fl oz) buttermilk
3 eggs, lightly whisked
2 tablespoons sweet chilli sauce
125 g (4 oz) butter, melted
½ cup (60 g/2 oz) grated Cheddar, plus extra for sprinkling

preparation: 15 minutes
cooking: 20 minutes
makes: 12

1 Preheat the oven to moderate 180°C (350°F/Gas 4). Lightly grease twelve ½-cup (125 ml/4 fl oz) muffin holes.

2 Sift the flour and polenta into a large bowl and make a well in the centre.

3 Place the buttermilk, eggs, sweet chilli sauce and melted butter in a small bowl and mix together thoroughly. Pour the liquid into the well in the dry ingredients, then add the grated Cheddar, season with salt and freshly ground black pepper and stir with a large spoon until just combined

4 Spoon the batter into the prepared muffin holes, sprinkle with a little extra grated Cheddar and bake for 15–20 minutes, or until golden and cooked through.

nutrition per cornbread
Fat 12.5 g; Protein 6.5 g; Carbohydrate 17.5 g; Dietary Fibre 1 g; Cholesterol 85 mg; 875 kJ (210 Cal)

shopping tip

Fine polenta is also known as fine semolina or cornmeal.
To make one large loaf, pour the batter into a greased 20 x 10 cm (8 x 4 inch) loaf tin, sprinkle with Cheddar and bake for an extra 15–20 minutes.
The cornbreads are perfect served warm with casseroles or stews to soak up the juices.

QUICK GREENS

english spinach

Wash 150 g (5 oz) baby English spinach leaves very well, then spin dry. Toss with one of the adjacent dressings, then serve.

serves 4

green beans

Top and tail 300 g (10 oz) green beans. Blanch in salted boiling water for 3–4 minutes, or until tender, but firm to the bite. Drain. Toss with one of the dressings, then serve.

serves 4

bok choy

Wash 4 heads of baby bok choy, then trim them and quarter them lengthways. Heat 2 teaspoons peanut oil in a hot wok or frying pan and stir-fry the bok choy over high heat for 2–3 minutes, or until just tender and wilted. Drizzle with one of the dressings, then serve.

serves 4

asparagus

Trim 250 g (8 oz) fresh asparagus. Toss with 1 tablespoon of olive oil, season well and roast on a baking tray for 15 minutes in a moderate (180°C/350°F/Gas 4) oven. Drizzle with one of the adjacent dressings, then serve.

serves 4

sesame and soy dressing

Combine 2 tablespoons soy sauce, 1 tablespoon each of chicken stock and toasted sesame seeds, 1 teaspoon finely julienned fresh ginger and ½ teaspoon sesame oil in a small jug and whisk together with a fork.

tahini dressing

Place 2 tablespoons seasoned rice vinegar, 1 tablespoon each of tahini and vegetable oil, 1 small clove crushed garlic, 1 teaspoon lime juice, ½ teaspoon sesame oil and a pinch of sugar in a small bowl and mix well.

thai dressing

Place ⅓ cup (80 ml/2¾ fl oz) lime juice, 2 tablespoons fish sauce, 2 tablespoons finely chopped fresh coriander leaves, 1 tablespoon grated palm sugar or soft brown sugar, 1 small, seeded fresh chopped red chilli and 1 small clove crushed garlic in a small jug and whisk together with a fork.

lemon and garlic dressing

Place ⅓ cup (80 ml/2¾ fl oz) olive oil, 2 tablespoons lemon juice, 1 tablespoon finely chopped fresh parsley, 1 teaspoon white wine vinegar, 1 teaspoon Dijon mustard, 2 cloves crushed garlic and a pinch of sugar in a small bowl and whisk together with a fork. Season with salt and pepper.

variation

You can use almost any greens in place of the ones we have suggested. Try broccoli, zucchini or any of the vast array of Asian greens now readily available at most supermarkets.

From left to right: English spinach with sesame and soy dressing, Green beans with tahini dressing, Bok choy with Thai dressing, Asparagus with lemon and garlic dressing.

242 red capsicum and basil loaf

ingredients

- 2 cups (250 g/8 oz) self-raising flour
- 1 teaspoon caster sugar
- 2 eggs
- 1 cup (250 ml/8 fl oz) milk
- 1/4 cup (60 ml/2 fl oz) olive oil
- 1 red capsicum, finely chopped
- 1/2 cup (50 g/1 3/4 oz) grated Parmesan
- 1/2 cup (30 g/1 oz) chopped fresh basil

preparation: 15 minutes
cooking: 40 minutes
serves: 4–6

1 Preheat the oven to moderately hot 200°C (400°F/Gas 6). Lightly grease a 10 x 20 cm (4 x 8 inch) loaf tin. Sift the flour and caster sugar into a large bowl. Place the eggs, milk and oil in a separate bowl and whisk together. Make a well in the centre of the flour mixture and pour in the milk mixture. Add the capsicum, Parmesan and basil, then season with salt and freshly ground black pepper. Stir until well combined.

2 Pour the batter into the prepared loaf tin and bake for about 40 minutes, or until a skewer inserted into the middle of the loaf comes out clean. Leave to cool in the tin for 5 minutes, then turn out. Serve warm.

nutrition per serve (6)
Fat 15 g; Protein 11.5 g; Carbohydrate 36.5 g; Dietary Fibre 2 g; Cholesterol 80 mg; 1370 kJ (325 Cal)

variation

Replace the red capsicum with finely chopped zucchini or carrot. If using zucchini, squeeze it dry to remove any excess liquid before adding to the flour.

This loaf is perfect when served with casseroles or stews to soak up the juices.

baby spinach and semi-dried tomato salad

ingredients

- ½ preserved lemon
- 150 g (5 oz) baby English spinach leaves
- 200 g (6½ oz) semi-dried tomatoes, sliced
- 225 g (7 oz) jar marinated artichoke hearts, drained and sliced
- ½ cup (85 g/3 oz) small black olives
- 2 tablespoons lemon juice
- ¼ cup (60 ml/2 fl oz) olive oil
- 1 large clove garlic, crushed

preparation: 15 minutes
cooking: nil
serves: 6

1 Remove and discard the pith and flesh from the preserved lemon. Wash the rind and thinly slice. Place the spinach leaves in a bowl with the sliced semi-dried tomatoes, artichoke hearts, olives and the preserved lemon slices.

2 Place the lemon juice, olive oil and garlic in a bowl, season with salt and freshly ground black pepper and mix well. Pour over the spinach mixture and toss to coat. Serve immediately.

nutrition per serve
Fat 10.5 g; Protein 3.5 g; Carbohydrate 10 g; Dietary Fibre 4 g; Cholesterol 0 mg; 615 kJ (145 Cal)

shopping tip

If you can't find semi-dried tomatoes, use sun-dried tomatoes or red capsicums.

desserts

256 individual baked cheesecakes

ingredients

4 butternut cookies
250 g (8 oz) cream cheese, softened
½ cup (125 g/4 oz) caster sugar
1 teaspoon grated lemon rind
1 tablespoon lemon juice
1 teaspoon vanilla essence
2 eggs, lightly beaten
mixed berries, to serve

preparation: 10 minutes
cooking: 20 minutes
serves: 4

1 Preheat the oven to moderate 180°C (350°F/Gas 4). Lightly grease four 1-cup (250 ml/8 fl oz) muffin holes and line the bases with baking paper.

2 Place a butternut cookie in the base of each muffin hole.

3 Using electric beaters, beat the cream cheese until smooth. Add the sugar, lemon rind, lemon juice and vanilla and beat until smooth. Gradually add the egg, beating well after each addition. Transfer the mixture to a jug for easier pouring, then pour into the muffin holes, leaving a 1 cm (½ inch) rim.

4 Bake for 20 minutes, or until set. Leave for 5 minutes, then run a flat-bladed knife around the side of each muffin hole and invert onto a plate. Remove the baking paper, turn upright and place a cake on each plate. Serve with berries.

nutrition per serve
Fat 26 g; Protein 9.5 g; Carbohydrate 45 g; Dietary Fibre 0.5 g; Cholesterol 153 mg; 1850 kJ (442 Cal)

serving tip

Drizzle melted dark chocolate over the top of the cheesecakes in a zigzag pattern.

champagne strawberries

ingredients

- 1/4 cup (60 g/2 oz) caster sugar
- 1 vanilla bean, split lengthways
- 300 ml (9 1/2 fl oz) Champagne
- 500 g (1 lb) fresh strawberries

preparation: 10 minutes
cooking: 5 minutes
serves: 4

1 Place the sugar, vanilla bean and Champagne in a saucepan and warm over low heat. Cook, stirring, for 3 minutes, or until the sugar has completely dissolved. Allow to cool slightly.

2 Put the strawberries in a serving bowl and pour the Champagne syrup over them, stirring gently to coat. Serve warm or refrigerate until cold, if preferred.

nutrition per serve
Fat 0 g; Protein 2 g; Carbohydrate 20 g; Dietary Fibre 3 g; Cholesterol 0 mg; 545 kJ (130 Cal)

serving tip

If you are entertaining, serve the strawberries in individual martini glasses with a couple of biscotti and a bowl of mascarpone for your guests to help themselves.

chocolate and croissant pudding

ingredients

- 3 eggs
- 1/4 cup (60 g/ 2 oz) caster sugar
- 1 1/4 cups (310 ml/10 fl oz) milk
- 3 plain croissants
- 100 g (3 1/42 oz) rum and raisin dark chocolate
- 1 tablespoon mixed peel
- 1 tablespoon demerara sugar

preparation: 15 minutes
cooking: 45 minutes
serves: 4–6

1 Preheat the oven to moderate 180°C (350°F/Gas 4). Grease a 1.25 litre rectangular ovenproof dish. Whisk together the eggs and caster sugar until the sugar dissolves, then whisk in the milk until fully combined and frothy.

2 Tear the croissants into small pieces and place half in the prepared dish. Roughly chop the chocolate and sprinkle it over the croissants, along with the mixed peel. Pour half the egg mixture over the croissants. Repeat with the remaining croissant pieces and egg mixture. Sprinkle the surface with demerara sugar.

3 Place the dish in a large deep baking tray. Pour in enough water to come halfway up the sides of the ovenproof dish and bake for 40–45 minutes, or until set and golden on top. Serve warm with ice cream.

nutrition per serve (6)
Fat 17.5 g; Protein 9 g; Carbohydrate 28.5 g; Dietary Fibre 2 g; Cholesterol 114 mg; 1280 kJ (305 Cal)

cooking hint

For an added chocolate bit, use chocolate croissants instead of plain ones.

lime delicious

ingredients

- 60 g (2 oz) softened unsalted butter
- 1/3 cup (75 g/2 1/2 oz) caster sugar
- 3 eggs, separated
- 1 1/2 teaspoons finely grated lime rind
- 1/4 cup (30 g/1 oz) self-raising flour
- 3/4 cup (185 ml/6 fl oz) milk
- 1/4 cup (60 ml/2 fl oz) lime juice

preparation: 15 minutes
cooking: 25 minutes
serves: 4

1 Preheat the oven to moderate 180°C (350°F/Gas 4) and lightly grease four 1-cup (250 ml/8 fl oz) ramekins. Beat the butter, sugar, egg yolks and lime rind together with electric beaters in a large bowl until light and creamy. Fold in the flour in two batches, alternating with the milk and lime juice.

2 In a clean, dry bowl, beat the egg whites until just stiff. Lightly fold into the batter, until just combined. Spoon into the ramekins and place them in a large, deep ovenproof dish. Pour in enough water to come halfway up the sides of the ramekins and bake for 25 minutes, or until risen and golden. Dust with icing sugar to serve.

nutrition per serve
Fat 18 g; Protein 7 g; Carbohydrate 26 g; Dietary Fibre 0.5 g; Cholesterol 179 mg; 1200 kJ (285 Cal)

variation

To make the classic lemon delicious pudding, simply replace the limes with lemons. To make this one large pudding, pour the mixture into a 1 litre ovenproof dish—you will need to increase the cooking time by 5–10 minutes.

apple crumble

ingredients

- 6 apples
- 1/3 cup (60 g/2 oz) soft brown sugar
- 2 cinnamon sticks
- 2 x 4 cm (3/4 x 1 1/2 inch) piece lemon rind
- 40 g (1 1/4 oz) unsalted butter, chopped
- 1/2 cup (60 g/2 oz) plain flour
- 2 tablespoons flaked almonds
- 1 teaspoon chopped unsalted butter, extra

preparation: 15 minutes
cooking: 25 minutes
serves: 4–6

1 Preheat the oven to moderately hot 200°C (400°F/Gas 6). Lightly grease a 1.25 litre ovenproof dish.

2 Peel, core and thinly slice the apples. Place the apple slices in a large saucepan with 1 tablespoon of the sugar, the cinnamon sticks, lemon rind and 1/2 cup (125 ml/4 fl oz) water. Simmer, partially covered, over medium heat for 8–10 minutes, or until the apples are tender but still holding their shape. Remove the cinnamon stick and lemon rind, then transfer the apples to the prepared dish.

3 To make the crumble mixture, place the chopped butter, flour and 1 tablespoon of the sugar in a small bowl. Mix with your fingertips, rubbing in the butter until it resembles coarse breadcrumbs. Mix in the flaked almonds until well coated.

4 Sprinkle the crumble mixture over the apples, dot with the extra butter and sprinkle with the remaining sugar. Bake for about 15 minutes, or until golden brown. Serve hot or cold, with custard or ice cream.

nutrition per serve (6)
Fat 9 g; Protein 2.5 g; Carbohydrate 33.5 g; Dietary Fibre 3.5 g; Cholesterol 19 mg; 910 kJ (215 Cal)

variation

Replace one of the apples with 150 g (5 oz) hulled, halved strawberries or 200 g (6 1/2 oz) fresh rhubarb cut into 4 cm (1 1/2 inch) lengths. Simmer for 8–10 minutes with the apple and continue as above.

ingredients

- ½ cup (125 ml/4 fl oz) golden syrup
- 2 teaspoons lemon juice
- 1 teaspoon grated lemon rind
- 15 cm (6 inch) ready-made cooked shortcrust pastry flan
- ½ teaspoon ground cinnamon
- ½ cup (25 g/¾ oz) fresh white breadcrumbs
- icing sugar, to dust

preparation: 10 minutes
cooking: 20 minutes
serves: 4

1 Preheat the oven to moderately hot 190°C (375°F/Gas 5). Place the syrup, lemon juice and rind in a small saucepan and warm over medium heat for 2 minutes, or until slightly runny.

2 Place the pastry flan on a baking tray and pour in half the syrup. Sprinkle with half of the combined cinnamon and breadcrumbs and pour on the remaining syrup. Sprinkle with the remaining crumb mixture.

3 Bake for 15 minutes, or until just set. Dust with icing sugar and serve.

nutrition per serve
Fat 12 g; Protein 4 g; Carbohydrate 57 g; Dietary Fibre 1 g; Cholesterol 13 mg; 1440 kJ (344 Cal)

serving tip

Although this tart is quite thin, it is rich enough that each person will need only a small piece.

red fruit salad with berries

To make the syrup, place ¼ cup (60 g/2 oz) caster sugar, ½ cup (125 ml/4 fl oz) red wine, 1 star anise, 1 teaspoon finely chopped lemon rind and ½ cup (125 ml/4 fl oz) water in a small saucepan. Bring to the boil over medium heat, stirring until the sugar is dissolved. Boil the syrup for 3 minutes, then set aside to cool for 30 minutes. When cool, strain the syrup into a bowl.

Mix together 250 g (8 oz) hulled and halved strawberries, 150 g (5 oz) blueberries, 150 g (5 oz) raspberries, mulberries or other red berries, 250 g (8 oz) cherries and 5 small pitted and quartered red plums in a large bowl. Pour on the red wine syrup, then mix well until the fruit is evenly coated in the syrup. Refrigerate for 1½ hours, then serve the fruit dressed with a little syrup and some plain yoghurt.

serves 6

banana and passionfruit salad with toasted coconut

Thinly slice 4 large ripe bananas on the diagonal. Toss the slices with 2 teaspoons lime or lemon juice and scatter on a serving plate. Drizzle with about 2 teaspoons honey and the pulp of 3 passionfruit. Sprinkle with 2 tablespoons toasted flaked coconut, then serve.

serves 4

melon with lemon grass syrup

Place ¼ cup (60 g/2 oz) caster sugar and 1 cup (250 ml/8 fl oz) water in a small saucepan. Heat over medium heat, stirring until the sugar has dissolved. Add 3 fresh kaffir lime leaves, 2 bruised stems lemon grass (white part only) and 2 thin slices fresh ginger. Simmer rapidly for 5–7 minutes, or until thickened. Allow to cool completely. Cut 250 g (8 oz) de-seeded and peeled watermelon, 250 g (8 oz) honeydew melon and 250 g (8 oz) rockmelon into 2 cm (¾ inch) cubes. Place the watermelon, honeydew and rockmelon in a large bowl with 12 peeled lychees.

Remove the lemon grass, ginger and lime leaves from the syrup and discard. Pour the syrup over the fruit and serve with ice cream.

serves 4

oranges with dates, mint and cinnamon

Cut the base off 5 oranges so that they can stand flat on their bases. Cut the rind off in a downward motion, cutting deep enough to remove all the white membrane. Slice the oranges thinly and place on a large flat serving dish with the slices slightly overlapping.

Combine the juice of another orange with 1½ teaspoons orange blossom water (optional) and pour over the orange slices. Thinly slice 5 fresh dates lengthways, then scatter over the oranges along with ¼ cup (30 g/1 oz) toasted slivered almonds, 1 tablespoon shredded fresh mint and ¼ teaspoon ground cinnamon.

serves 4

From left to right: Red fruit salad with berries, Banana and passionfruit salad with toasted coconut, Melon with lemon grass syrup, Oranges with dates, mint and cinnamon.

cooking hint

The best guide to making a sensational fruit salad is to use fruits that are in season. Not only will they taste better, they will also be a lot cheaper than fruits out of season.

268 marsala zabaglione with grilled plums

ingredients

Zabaglione
- 4 egg yolks
- 1/4 cup (60 g/2 oz) caster sugar
- 1/3 cup (80 ml/2 3/4 fl oz) Marsala

- 4 plums
- 1 tablespoon caster sugar, extra

preparation: 5 minutes
cooking: 10 minutes
serves: 4

1 To make the zabaglione, half fill a saucepan with water and bring to simmering point. Place the egg yolks, sugar and Marsala in a bowl, whisk together and place over the saucepan, ensuring the water doesn't come into contact with the base of the bowl. Whisk for 5 minutes over the simmering water, or until frothy and thickened and the whisk leaves a trail.

2 Cut the plums in half and remove the stones. Place the plums cut-side-up on a grill tray and sprinkle with the extra sugar. Grill for 5 minutes, or until the tops are caramelized and the plums are tender. Serve drizzled with the Marsala zabaglione.

nutrition per serve
Fat 5 g; Protein 3 g; Carbohydrate 36 g; Dietary Fibre 2 g; Cholesterol 178 mg; 969 kJ (232 Cal)

variation

This recipe is also delicious with peaches or nectarines. For the best results, choose stone fruit that is perfectly ripe.

chocolate rice pudding

ingredients

1 cup (220 g/7 oz) medium-grain rice
3 cups (750 ml/24 fl oz) milk
125 g (4 oz) good-quality dark chocolate, chopped into small pieces
2–3 tablespoons Kahlua
1–2 tablespoons caster sugar
thick cream, to serve

preparation: 10 minutes
cooking: 30 minutes
serves: 6

1 Place the rice in a saucepan, add 2 cups (500 ml/16 fl oz) boiling water and stir until well combined. Boil, stirring occasionally, for 5 minutes, or until the water is nearly absorbed. Add the milk and bring to the boil. Reduce the heat and simmer, covered, over very low heat for 20 minutes, or until the rice is cooked and the pudding is thick and creamy. Do not let the pudding bubble over.

2 Add the chocolate and Kahlua, and stir until the chocolate is melted and well combined. Add 1–2 tablespoons caster sugar, to taste. Spoon into six ¾-cup (185 ml/6 fl oz) ramekins and serve with thick cream.

nutrition per serve
Fat 11 g; Protein 7.5 g; Carbohydrate 55 g; Dietary Fibre 1 g; Cholesterol 17 mg; 1490 kJ (356 Cal)

cooking hint

Stir the rice once or twice with a wooden spoon during cooking to make sure that it is not catching on the bottom and burning. If it has begun to 'catch', transfer the rice to a bowl, wash the pan and return the rice to the heat in the clean pan.

272 apricot fool

ingredients

- 200 g ($6\frac{1}{2}$ oz) dried apricots
- large strip of lemon peel, pith removed
- 300 ml ($9\frac{1}{2}$ fl oz) cream
- $1\frac{1}{2}$ tablespoons caster sugar
- 1 teaspoon lemon juice

preparation: 15 minutes
cooking: 15 minutes
serves: 4–6

1 Place the apricots, lemon peel and 1 cup (250 ml/8 fl oz) water in a small saucepan. Simmer for 15 minutes, or until the apricots are plump.
2 Meanwhile, pour the cream into a bowl and, using electric beaters, whip until soft peaks form.
3 Add the sugar and lemon juice to the apricots and stir well. Remove the lemon peel. Place in a food processor or blender and process until puréed, then transfer to a metal or glass bowl and sit over iced water to quickly cool the apricot mixture. Stir frequently until cool.
4 Gently fold in the whipped cream and spoon the mixture into tumblers. Delicious served with wafers.

nutrition per serve (6)
Fat 21 g; Protein 2.5 g; Carbohydrate 21 g; Dietary Fibre 3 g; Cholesterol 68 mg; 1185 kJ (283 Cal)

variation

For a delicious mango fool, purée 3 large ripe mangoes and 1 cup (250 g/8 oz) of ready-made custard in a food processor or blender until smooth, then gently fold in $1\frac{2}{3}$ cups (410 ml/13 fl oz) whipped cream.

quick lemon meringue pie

ingredients

- 155 g (5 oz) jar lemon butter or curd
- 18 cm (7 inch) ready-made cooked shortcrust pastry flan
- 2 egg whites
- 1/2 cup (125 g/4 oz) caster sugar

preparation: 20 minutes
cooking: 10 minutes
serves: 4

1 Preheat the oven to moderately hot 200°C (400°F/Gas 6). Spoon an even layer of the lemon butter over the pastry case, spreading right to the edge. Smooth the top with a flat-bladed knife.

2 Whisk the egg whites in a clean, dry bowl until soft peaks form. Gradually add the sugar, beating well after each addition until stiff and glossy peaks form.

3 Cover the lemon butter with the egg whites, forming peaks. Place the flan on a baking tray and bake for 8–10 minutes, or until the peaks have turned light golden.

nutrition per serve
Fat 20 g; Protein 5.5 g; Carbohydrate 70 g; Dietary Fibre 0.5 g; Cholesterol 51 mg; 1950 kJ (466 Cal)

variation

Ready-made shortcrust pastry flans are extremely versatile and can be filled with almost anything. Try whipped mascarpone and drained canned fruits.

mixed berry millefeuille

ingredients

1 sheet ready-rolled puff pastry, thawed
150 g (5 oz) sour cream
2 tablespoons soft brown sugar
2 tablespoons cream
200 g (6½ oz) mixed fresh or frozen berries
icing sugar, to dust

preparation: 20 minutes
cooking: 10 minutes
serves: 4

1 Preheat the oven to moderately hot 200°C (400°F/Gas 6). Line a baking tray with baking paper.

2 Cut the pastry sheet into eight 6 x 12 cm (2½ x 4¾ inch) rectangles. Place the pastry pieces on the prepared tray and bake for 10 minutes, or until the pastry is puffed and lightly golden. Set aside to cool. (If you lightly flatten the puffs with your hand, the cream will sit better.)

3 Place the sour cream, soft brown sugar and cream in a bowl and beat until stiff peaks form. Divide into four portions and spoon one portion each onto the flat side of four of the pastry puffs. Top with the mixed berries and cover with the four pastry tops, puffed-side-up. Dust generously with icing sugar and serve immediately, with extra berries, if desired.

nutrition per serve
Fat 30 g; Protein 4 g; Carbohydrate 30 g; Dietary Fibre 2.5 g; Cholesterol 73 mg; 1650 kJ (395 Cal)

variation

The millefeuille is a simple idea that can be adapted to whatever fruits are in season. Use passionfruit, sliced peaches, mangoes or stewed rhubarb.

biscotti and coffee parfait

ingredients

- 1 cup (250 ml/8 fl oz) cream
- 1 tablespoon soft brown sugar
- 1 tablespoon Kahlua
- 8 scoops coffee ice cream
- 150 g (5 oz) almond biscotti, chopped
- 1/3 cup (50 g/1 3/4 oz) Vienna almonds, chopped

preparation: 15 minutes
cooking: nil
serves: 4

1 Pour the cream into a large bowl, add the sugar and whisk until the cream has thickened slightly. Add the Kahlua and whisk again until well mixed together.
2 Line four parfait glasses or 1 1/2 cup (375 ml/12 fl oz) glass tumblers in front of you and place one scoop of ice cream into the bottom of each one. Divide half of the chopped biscotti among the glasses, then add 1 1/2 tablespoons of the Kahlua-cream mixture.
3 Top with the remaining biscotti, 1 1/2 tablespoons of the cream mixture and a final scoop of the ice cream. Sprinkle with the chopped Vienna almonds and serve immediately before the ice cream melts.

nutrition per serve
Fat 45 g; Protein 7 g; Carbohydrate 42 g; Dietary Fibre 1.5 g; Cholesterol 111 mg; 2512 kJ (600 Cal)

variation

This recipe can be adapted to suit almost any flavours. Try a combination of Frangelico with hazelnut ice cream and hazelnut biscotti, or rum with rum and raisin ice cream.
If you are making this dessert for children, omit the liqueur and replace it with a little vanilla essence or other flavoured syrup that complements the flavours.

278 rhubarb meringue

ingredients

- 1 kg (2 lb) rhubarb, trimmed and cut into 2 cm (3/4 inch) pieces
- 1/3 cup (90 g/3 oz) caster sugar, or to taste
- 3 egg whites
- 1/3 cup (90 g/3 oz) caster sugar, extra
- 2 tablespoons flaked almonds

preparation: 10 minutes
cooking: 20 minutes
serves: 4

1 Preheat the oven to moderately hot 200°C (400°F/Gas 6). Place the rhubarb, sugar and 2 tablespoons water in a saucepan and bring to the boil. Reduce the heat and simmer, covered, for 5–8 minutes, stirring occasionally, until the rhubarb is tender. Transfer to a deep 2 litre round ovenproof dish.

2 Using electric beaters, whisk the egg whites in a clean, dry bowl until soft peaks form. Gradually add the extra sugar, beating well after each addition until stiff and glossy peaks form.

3 Cover the fruit with the egg whites, creating soft peaks, then scatter the almonds over the top and bake for 10 minutes, or until the meringue is lightly golden on the peaks. Serve warm.

nutrition per serve
Fat 4.5 g; Protein 8 g; Carbohydrate 50 g; Dietary Fibre 8.5 g; Cholesterol 0 mg; 1138 kJ (272 Cal)

cooking hint

Try not to stir the rhubarb too vigorously or it will break up and lose its texture.

rice pudding with mixed berries

ingredients

- 1 cup (220 g/7 oz) short-grain rice
- 1/2 cup (125 g/4 oz) plain yoghurt
- 300 ml (9 1/2 fl oz) cream
- 1/3 cup (90 g/3 oz) caster sugar
- 1 teaspoon vanilla essence
- 250 g (8 oz) fresh strawberries, hulled and sliced
- 300 g (10 oz) fresh or frozen blueberries
- 1 tablespoon caster sugar, extra

preparation: 10 minutes
cooking: 20 minutes
serves: 4

1 Place the rice, 1/2 teaspoon salt and 2 1/2 cups (625 ml/20 fl oz) water in a saucepan and bring to the boil, stirring once. Reduce the heat and simmer, covered, for 20 minutes, or until soft and tender but still moist. Leave for 5 minutes.
2 Meanwhile, put the yoghurt, cream, sugar and vanilla in a large bowl and whisk together until the sugar dissolves.
3 Toss together the berries and extra sugar. Cover and refrigerate until ready to serve.
4 Add the hot rice to the cream mixture. Add milk or extra cream if the mixture is too thick. Divide among four bowls, top with the berries and serve.

nutrition per serve
Fat 33 g; Protein 8 g; Carbohydrate 84 g; Dietary Fibre 4 g; Cholesterol 105 mg; 2790 kJ (668 Cal)

cooking hint

If you have to refrigerate the rice pudding, it will thicken—use cream or milk to thin it to the desired consistency.

toasted madeira cake with peppered oranges

ingredients

110 g (3 1/2 oz) sugar
1/4 teaspoon freshly ground black peppercorns
4 wide strips orange peel, pith removed
2 navel oranges, skin and pith removed, each cut into 4 rounds
450 g (14 oz) Madeira cake, cut into four 2 cm (3/4 inch) slices
1/3 cup (80 ml/2 3/4 fl oz) olive oil
250 g (8 oz) mascarpone

preparation: 15 minutes
cooking: 15 minutes
serves: 4

1 Place the sugar, peppercorns, orange peel and 1 cup (250 ml/ 8 fl oz) water in a saucepan and stir over low heat for several minutes, or until the sugar dissolves. Increase the heat to medium and simmer rapidly for 10 minutes, or until thick and syrupy. Add the orange slices and cook, covered, for 2 minutes. Remove from the heat and keep warm.

2 Meanwhile, brush both sides of the cake slices liberally with the olive oil and toast under a hot grill for 3–5 minutes each side, or until golden brown all over. Keep warm.

3 Place the cake slices on four warmed serving plates. Top each piece with two orange slices and a spoonful of the syrup. Add a dollop of mascarpone and serve immediately.

nutrition per serve
Fat 57 g; Protein 15 g; Carbohydrate 87 g; Dietary Fibre 2.5 g; Cholesterol 145 mg; 3784 kJ (905 Cal)

cooking hint

Unusual as it may seem, the pepper in this recipe marries well with the other ingredients, so don't be tempted to omit it.

ingredients

60 g (2 oz) unsalted butter
1/4 cup (45 g/1 1/2 oz) soft brown sugar
6 fresh figs, halved
thick cream or ice cream, to serve

preparation: 5 minutes
cooking: 10 minutes
serves: 4

1 To make the caramel sauce, place the butter and sugar in a small saucepan, and stir for 2–3 minutes, or until the butter melts and the sugar dissolves.

2 Brush some of the caramel sauce over the cut side of the figs. Grill for 3–5 minutes, or until soft, brushing with the remaining caramel or spoon it on during cooking. Serve with any remaining sauce and a dollop of thick cream or ice cream.

nutrition per serve
Fat 12 g; Protein 1 g; Carbohydrate 16 g; Dietary Fibre 1.5 g; Cholesterol 38 mg; 733 kJ (175 Cal)

cooking hint

If you prefer a runnier sauce, add a little cream to the caramel after basting the figs.

chocolate cherry parfait

Drain a 400 g (13 oz) can pitted black cherries. Fill four parfait glasses with 1–2 scoops chocolate ice cream. Divide the cherries among the glasses, then top with 1–2 scoops of lamington or choc chip-flavoured ice cream. Drizzle each glass with 1 tablespoon good-quality chocolate sauce and garnish with chopped, dark chocolate cherry bar.

serves 4

crunchy vanilla ice cream log

Lightly grease a chilled 25 x 7.5 x 4 cm (10 x 3 x 1 1/2 inch) bar tin and line it with plastic wrap, leaving enough plastic wrap to overhang the long sides of the tin. Spoon half of a 500 g (1 lb) tub of slightly softened good-quality vanilla ice cream into the tin, pressing down firmly to make sure the corners are filled. Sprinkle a chopped 80 g (2 3/4 oz) chocolate honeycomb confectionery bar evenly over the ice cream. Cover with the remaining ice cream, pressing the top down firmly and smoothing with a flat-bladed knife. Fold the overhanging ends of the plastic wrap so that it covers the ice cream and freeze for at least 25 minutes. To serve, quickly dip the tin into a basin full of hot water and lift the log out, using the plastic wrap to help you. Cut the log into approximately 3 cm (1 1/4 inch) slices and serve immediately.

serves 4–6

From left to right: Chocolate cherry parfait, Crunchy vanilla ice cream log, Banana caramel ice cream stack, Affogato.

banana caramel ice cream stack

Cut 400 g (13 oz) pound cake into 1.5 cm (5/8 inch) thick slices. You will need eight slices. (Any leftover cake may be frozen and used at a later date.) Place one slice of cake on each of four serving plates. Cut 2 large bananas into 1 cm (1/2 inch) diagonal slices. Top each cake slice with individual, rectangular, vanilla ice cream slabs, then the banana slices. Pour 3 tablespoons caramel sauce over the bananas and scatter with chopped, honey-roasted macadamia nuts. Top with the remaining cake slices, then drizzle with extra caramel sauce (drizzle some on the plate as well as the stack). Top with extra honey-roasted macadamias and serve immediately.

serves 4

affogato

Place a large scoop of good-quality vanilla ice cream in four coffee cups or small bowls and pour a shot of hot espresso over each scoop. For an added kick, drizzle with your favourite liqueur, such as amaretto, frangelico or cognac.

serves 4

cooking hint

Don't let the ice cream soften too much or it won't re-freeze hard enough to serve in the time given.

For a rippled effect for the ice cream log, try using chocolate and vanilla ice cream and press them into the tin in alternate layers, with the chocolate honeycomb in the centre of the two layers.

284 chocolate pancakes with choc-cherry sauce

ingredients

- 425 g (14 oz) can pitted black cherries
- 100 ml (3½ fl oz) cream
- 200 g (6½ oz) dark chocolate, chopped
- 1 cup (125 g/4 oz) self-raising flour
- ¼ cup (30 g/1 oz) cocoa powder
- ¼ cup (60 g/2 oz) caster sugar
- ½ teaspoon bicarbonate of soda
- 1⅓ cups (350 ml/11 fl oz) milk
- 1 egg, lightly beaten
- ½ teaspoon vanilla essence
- 40 g (1¼ oz) unsalted butter, chopped
- 6 scoops vanilla ice cream

preparation: 10 minutes
cooking: 20 minutes
serves: 6

1 To make the sauce, drain the cherries, reserving 2 tablespoons of the syrup. Place the cream and chocolate in a heatproof bowl. Bring a saucepan of water to the boil, then remove the pan from the heat. Sit the bowl over the pan, making sure the base of the bowl does not sit in the water. Stir occasionally until the chocolate has melted and combined with the cream. Stir in the cherries and reserved syrup. Keep warm.

2 To make the pancakes, sift the flour and cocoa into a bowl and stir in the sugar and bicarbonate of soda. Make a well in the centre and gradually add the combined milk, egg and vanilla, mixing until smooth.

3 Melt some of the butter in a frying pan over medium heat. Pour ⅓ cup (80 ml/2¾ fl oz) of the batter into the pan and swirl gently to make a 12 cm (4½ inch) pancake. Cook for 1–2 minutes, or until bubbles form on the surface and the underside is golden brown. Turn over and cook for 30 seconds more, or until golden. Transfer to a plate and keep warm. Repeat with the remaining batter to make five more pancakes, adding more butter as needed.

4 Place a scoop of ice cream on one half of each pancake and fold the other half over. Drizzle with the sauce and serve immediately.

nutrition per serve
Fat 27 g; Protein 8.5 g; Carbohydrate 58 g; Dietary Fibre 2.5 g; Cholesterol 60 mg; 2110 kJ (503 Cal)

cooking hint

Add a little milk if the batter thickens on standing—the consistency should be like thick pouring cream.

coconut lime ice cream

ingredients

- 1/4 cup (25 g/3/4 oz) desiccated coconut
- 1 1/2 tablespoons grated lime rind
- 1/3 cup (80 ml/2 3/4 fl oz) lime juice
- 1/3 cup (35 g/1 1/4 oz) coconut milk powder
- 1 litre good-quality vanilla ice cream, softened
- coconut macaroons, to serve

preparation: 10 minutes + 30 minutes freezing
cooking: nil
serves: 4

1 Place the desiccated coconut, grated lime rind, lime juice and coconut milk powder in a bowl, and mix together well.

2 Add the coconut mixture to the ice cream and fold through with a large metal spoon until evenly incorporated. Work quickly so that the ice cream does not melt. Return the mixture to the freezer and freeze for 30 minutes to firm it up. To serve, place 3 scoops of the ice cream in four latté glasses and serve with some coconut macaroons on the side.

nutrition per serve
Fat 19.5 g; Protein 5 g; Carbohydrate 19 g; Dietary Fibre 1.5 g; Cholesterol 30 mg; 1230 kJ (293 Cal)

cooking hint

Try not to allow the ice cream to melt too much when folding in the coconut or it will have an icy texture when re-frozen. You can replace the lime with lemon or orange.

286 plum crumble cake

ingredients

- 3/4 cup (165 g/5 1/2 oz) demerara sugar
- 2 cups (250 g/8 oz) self-raising flour
- 150 g (5 oz) unsalted butter
- 1 egg
- 825 g (1 lb 11 oz) can plums in syrup, drained and thinly sliced
- 1 1/2 teaspoons ground cinnamon
- 2/3 cup (100 g/3 1/2 oz) blanched almonds, chopped

preparation: 15 minutes
cooking: 50 minutes
serves: 8

1 Preheat the oven to moderate 180°C (350°F/Gas 4). Grease a 20 cm (8 inch) shallow sandwich tin and line the base with baking paper. Place the sugar, flour and butter in a food processor and process in short bursts until the mixture is combined and crumbly.

2 Add the egg and process until well combined. Press half the mixture onto the base of the prepared tin. Arrange the plum slices evenly over the dough, then sprinkle with the cinnamon.

3 Knead the almonds lightly into the remaining dough, then press onto the plum layer. Bake for 50 minutes, or until a skewer comes out clean when inserted into the centre of the cake. Leave in the tin for 15 minutes before carefully turning out onto a wire rack to cool slightly. Delicious served warm with thick cream.

nutrition per serve
Fat 23.5 g; Protein 7 g; Carbohydrate 57 g; Dietary Fibre 4 g; Cholesterol 69.5 mg; 1935 kJ (460 Cal)

variation

You can make individual cakes by dividing the batter among four lightly greased 3/4 cup (185 ml/6 fl oz) ramekins—check them after 40 minutes cooking time.

white chocolate berry crunch

ingredients

90 g (3 oz) coconut macaroons, lightly crushed
150 g (5 oz) white chocolate, chopped into even-sized pieces
300 ml (9½ fl oz) cream
250 g (8 oz) fresh or frozen raspberries
50 g (1¾ oz) slivered almonds, toasted

preparation: 20 minutes
cooking: 5 minutes
serves: 4

1 Divide the crushed macaroons among four parfait glasses or 1½-cup (375 ml/12 fl oz) tumblers.
2 Place the chocolate in a heatproof bowl. Bring a saucepan of water to the boil, then remove from the heat. Sit the bowl over the saucepan, making sure the base of the bowl does not sit in the water. Stir occasionally until the chocolate has melted. Cool slightly.
3 Using electric beaters, whip the cream until soft peaks form, then gently fold in the melted chocolate. Divide half the chocolate-cream mixture among the glasses, top with the raspberries, then cover with the remaining chocolate-cream mixture. Sprinkle with toasted slivered almonds and serve.

nutrition per serve
Fat 55 g; Protein 9 g; Carbohydrate 43 g; Dietary Fibre 7 g; Cholesterol 111 mg; 2898 kJ (692 Cal)

variation

Use lightly crushed vanilla or chocolate wafers instead of the macaroons and toss the berries in a little liqueur such as amaretto or frangelico before placing in the glasses.

fruit toasts

ingredients

unsalted butter, to spread
8 slices day-old bread
1 tablespoon caster sugar
1/2 teaspoon ground cinnamon
300 g (10 oz) mixed fresh berries
maple syrup, to serve

preparation: 15 minutes
cooking: 5 minutes
serves: 4

1 Butter both sides of the bread slices. Put the caster sugar and cinnamon in a small bowl and mix together. Sprinkle one side of each piece of bread with the cinnamon sugar.

2 Put four bread slices in a jaffle maker, cinnamon-side-down.

3 Spoon a quarter of the berries on each slice of bread in the jaffle maker. Cover with a second piece of bread, cinnamon-side-up, and cook for 2 minutes, or until golden brown. Cut off the crusts, if desired. Serve with a drizzle of maple syrup.

nutrition per serve
Fat 8 g; Protein 5.5 g; Carbohydrate 42 g; Dietary Fibre 4 g; Cholesterol 20 mg; 1088 kJ (260 Cal)

variation

For added richness, use sliced brioche instead of the bread—the butter and eggs in brioche give it a cake-like texture.

individual banana pies

ingredients

4 sheets ready-rolled shortcrust pastry
1 tablespoon demerara sugar
1/4 teaspoon ground cinnamon
4 bananas

preparation: 10 minutes
cooking: 20 minutes
serves: 4

1 Preheat the oven to hot 220°C (425°F/Gas 7). Lightly grease two baking trays. Cut one 17 cm (7 inch) circle out of each sheet of pastry, using a plate as a guide.

2 Place the sugar and cinnamon in a small bowl and mix together.

3 Thinly slice each banana on the diagonal and place one sliced banana in the centre of each pastry circle, leaving a 3 cm (1 1/4 inch) border. Sprinkle with the combined sugar and cinnamon.

4 Fold the edges of the pastry to slightly enclose the filling, leaving a gap in the centre. Place on the baking trays and cook for about 20 minutes, or until the pastry is crisp and golden. Serve warm with cream or vanilla ice cream.

nutrition per serve
Fat 38 g; Protein 12 g; Carbohydrate 97 g; Dietary Fibre 6 g; Cholesterol 42 mg; 3240 kJ (774 Cal)

variation

These pies can be made with almost any fruit, fresh or canned. If you use canned fruit, drain it very well before putting it on the pastry to prevent the pastry from becoming soggy.

290 chocolate shortbread stacks

ingredients

- 1½ cups (185 g/6 oz) plain flour
- ⅓ cup (40 g/1¼ oz) cocoa powder
- ¾ cup (90 g/3 oz) icing sugar
- 225 g (7 oz) chilled unsalted butter, chopped
- 2 egg yolks
- 1 teaspoon vanilla essence
- 1 cup (250 ml/8 fl oz) double thick cream
- 250 g (8 oz) strawberries, quartered
- cocoa powder, to dust
- icing sugar, to dust

Berry sauce

- 250 g (8 oz) fresh or frozen (thawed) strawberries
- 1 tablespoon caster sugar

preparation: 15 minutes
cooking: 15 minutes
serves: 6

1 Preheat the oven to hot 210°C (415°F/Gas 6–7). Line two baking trays with baking paper. Sift the flour, cocoa and icing sugar into a large bowl. Rub the butter in with your fingertips until the mixture resembles fine breadcrumbs. Add the yolks and vanilla and mix with a knife until the mixture comes together. Turn out onto a lightly floured surface and form into a ball.

2 Roll the pastry out between two layers of baking paper to about 5 mm (¼ inch) thick. Using a 7 cm (2¾ inch) fluted round cutter, cut out 18 rounds. Place on the baking trays and bake for 10–12 minutes, or until cooked through. Transfer to a wire rack to cool.

3 Meanwhile, to make the berry sauce, process the strawberries and sugar until smooth, then stir in 1–2 tablespoons water until the sauce is pourable.

4 Place a shortbread on a serving plate and cover with some cream and strawberries. Top with a second shortbread, more cream and strawberries, then finish with a third shortbread. Repeat, making five more stacks. Dust with icing sugar and serve with the sauce.

nutrition per serve
Fat 52 g; Protein 7 g; Carbohydrate 42 g; Dietary Fibre 2.5 g; Cholesterol 211 mg; 2739 kJ (654 Cal)

storage hint

Any leftover shortbreads will keep in an airtight container for up to 1 week.

individual sticky date puddings

ingredients

- 1½ cups (270 g/9 oz) pitted dates, chopped
- 1 teaspoon bicarbonate of soda
- 1 teaspoon vanilla essence
- 60 g (2 oz) unsalted butter
- 1½ cups (185 g/6 oz) self-raising flour
- ⅔ cup (125 g/4 oz) soft brown sugar
- 2 eggs

Sauce

- 90 g (3 oz) unsalted butter
- ¾ cup (140 g/4½ oz) soft brown sugar
- 2 tablespoons golden syrup
- ¾ cup (185 ml/6 fl oz) cream

preparation: 10 minutes
cooking: 25 minutes
serves: 6

1 Preheat the oven to moderate 180°C (350°F/Gas 4). Lightly grease six 1 cup (250 ml/8 fl oz) muffin holes. Put the dates and 1 cup (250 ml/8 fl oz) water in a small saucepan, bring to the boil, then remove from the heat and stir in the bicarbonate of soda and vanilla. Add the butter and stir until dissolved.

2 Sift the flour into a large bowl, add the sugar and stir. Make a well in the centre, add the date mixture and eggs and mix. Spoon the mixture evenly into the prepared holes and bake for 20 minutes, or until a skewer comes out clean when inserted into the centre.

3 Meanwhile, to make the sauce, place all the ingredients in a saucepan and stir over low heat for 3–4 minutes, or until the sugar dissolves. Bring to the boil, then reduce the heat and simmer for 2 minutes. To serve, turn the puddings out onto serving plates, drizzle with the sauce and serve with ice cream.

nutrition per serve
Fat 35 g; Protein 6 g; Carbohydrate 105 g; Dietary Fibre 5.5 g; Cholesterol 136 mg; 3085 kJ (737 Cal)

variation

For added texture, replace ½ cup (80 g/2¾ oz) of the dates with ½ cup (60 g/2 oz) chopped walnuts.

Arborio rice is a special short-grain rice used for making risotto.

Balsamic vinegar is a rich, sweet and fragrant vinegar originating from Modena in Italy. Often used in dressings.

Basmati rice is a special rice often used in Indian cooking. It has a nutty flavour. Available in supermarkets.

Bicarbonate of soda (baking soda)

Black beans are fermented and heavily salted black soy beans. Rinse thoroughly before use. Available canned or in packets.

Bocconcini are small balls of fresh Italian mozzarella available from delicatessens. Keep refrigerated and covered in the whey in which they are sold for up to 3 weeks. Discard if they show signs of yellowing.

Bok choy (Chinese chard, Chinese white cabbage) is a popular Asian green vegetable. The smaller type is called baby bok choy or Shanghai bok choy.

Cannellini beans (white beans, Italian white beans) are available canned or dried.

Capsicums (peppers)

Caster sugar (superfine sugar) is a fine white sugar with very small crystals.

Cellophane noodles (glass noodles, dried bean thread vermicelli, mung bean thread vermicelli) are thin, dried transparent noodles made from mung bean flour. They are usually soaked in warm water.

Chilli bean paste (chilli bean sauce) is made from fermented soy beans and is available from Asian food stores.

Chinese barbecued pork (char siu) is a marinated pork fillet that has been barbecued over charcoal. Available from Chinese barbecue shops.

Chinese broccoli (gai larn) has smooth, round stems and large dark green leaves. The juicy stems, trimmed of most of their leaves, are the part of the plant most commonly eaten.

Chinese dried mushrooms (Chinese dried black mushrooms) have a distinctive woody, smoky flavour which is intensified by the drying process. Rehydrate before using them.

Chorizo is a spicy sausage flavoured with paprika and sold either fresh or as a hard cured sausage to be eaten cold.

Choy sum (flowering cabbage) is an Asian green with edible stems and leaves. Available from greengrocers.

Clarified butter is butter which has had the milk solids removed, enabling it to withstand high temperatures during cooking.

Coconut cream and milk are extracted from the flesh of fresh coconuts. The cream is thick and almost spreadable. The milk is extracted after the cream has been pressed and is thinner.

Coriander (cilantro, Chinese parsley). All parts of this aromatic plant—seeds, leaves, stem and root—can be eaten.

Cornflour (cornstarch) is a fine white powder that is usually used as a thickening agent.

Couscous is a cereal processed from semolina and generally associated with North African cuisine. Instant couscous takes only 10 minutes to prepare.

Curry leaves are small and pointed leaves with a spicy fragrance, available fresh and dried from Asian food stores.

Dashi powder is made from dried kelp (kombu) and dried fish (bonito) and is the basic stock used in Japanese cooking. It is available as granules or as a powder which needs to be dissolved in hot water. It is available from Asian food stores.

Desiccated coconut is the dried finely processed flesh of the coconut, often used in baking. Shredded and flaked coconut is sweeter and moister.

Eggplants (aubergines) come in a variety of shapes, sizes and colours. Slender eggplants are also called baby or Japanese eggplants, while the most commonly used are larger and rounder.

English spinach (spinach) is sometimes confused with Swiss chard but is much more tender and delicate. Requires little to no cooking but should be washed several times to remove dirt.

Fish sauce is a brown, salty sauce with a characteristic 'fishy' smell. It is made from small fish that have been fermented in the sun. It is a popular seasoning in Southeast Asian cuisine. Use it sparingly as it has a strong flavour.

Flat-leaf parsley (Italian parsley, Continental parsley)

French shallots are members of the onion family but have a sweeter flavour.

Fresh rice sheet noodles are flat, white noodles made from rice flour that are steamed and lightly oiled before being packaged. Rinse in hot water to loosen and separate them before use. Do not store in the refrigerator or they will go hard and be difficult to separate.

Garam masala is an Indian spice blend and is available ready-made from delicatessens and some supermarkets.

Ginger is a fragrant, spicy root which is indispensable in Asian cooking. The brown skin is usually peeled off before use. Ground ginger cannot be adequately substituted for fresh.

Goat's cheese is available in a variety of shapes, sizes and degrees of maturation. Chèvre is the term for fresh goat's cheese, which is the one most commonly used in cooking because of its mild flavour.

Golden syrup (light treacle, light molasses) is collected at the end of the cane sugar refining process.

Green beans (French beans, string beans)

Hoisin sauce is a sweet, thick sauce made from fermented soy beans, flavoured with garlic and five-spice powder. Available in supermarkets.

Icing sugar (confectioners' sugar, powdered sugar). Made by grinding granulated sugar to a fine powder.

Japanese curry comes in a solid block or in powder form and is available in Asian supermarkets.

Japanese soy sauce is less salty and much lighter and sweeter than regular soy. Because it is naturally brewed it must be refrigerated after opening.

Jasmine rice is a fragrant long-grain rice often used in Asian cooking.

Kaffir lime leaves are fragrant leaves from the kaffir lime tree. Each leaf is shaped in a figure eight—in our recipes, half of the figure of eight represents one leaf. Available fresh and dried from some greengrocers and supermarkets.

Kecap manis is a thick, sweet soy sauce. If unavailable, use regular soy sauce sweetened with a little soft brown sugar.

Lamb backstraps (lamb loin fillets)

Lemon grass is a thick-stemmed herb with pale leaves. It has a lemony flavour and aroma. Trim the base, remove the tough outer layers and finely chop the inner white stem.

Mascarpone cheese is a soft fresh cheese made with cream to which citric or tartaric acid has been added.

Mirin is a sweetened rice wine and is available from Asian food stores. There is no real substitute.

Miso paste is made from cooked, mashed, salted, fermented soy beans and grains. It varies in colour from yellow to brown; the darker the colour the saltier and more pungent the taste.

Nori is dried seaweed that comes in sheets, either plain or roasted. Quick toasting over a naked flame freshens the nori and produces a nutty flavour.

Olive oil comes in different varieties suitable for different purposes. Extra virgin or virgin olive oil are most commonly used in dressings. Regular olive oils are preferred for cooking because of their neutral flavour. Light olive oil refers to the low content of extra virgin olive oil rather than lightness of calories.

Oyster sauce is a thick, smooth brown sauce with a rich slightly sweet flavour. Although it is made from oysters and soy sauce, it does not taste fishy.

Palm sugar is a rich, aromatic sugar which is available in block form in Asian food stores. If unavailable, substitute soft brown sugar.

Pancetta is meat from the belly of a pig that has been cured in salt and spices. Usually sold rolled into a sausage shape and cut into very thin slices.

Parmesan is a hard cow's milk cheese used widely in Italian cooking. Sold either grated or in blocks, freshly grated has a much better flavour.

Peanut oil (groundnut oil) can tolerate high heat so is ideal for deep-frying.

Plain flour (all-purpose flour)

Polenta (cornmeal) is ground dried corn kernels.

Prawns (shrimp) are crustaceans which come in various sizes and colours. They become opaque and turn pink once cooked.

Prosciutto is an Italian ham that has been cured by salting then drying in the air. It does not require cooking.

Rice vinegar is a clear, pale yellow, mild and sweet-tasting vinegar made from fermented rice.

Rocket (arugula, rugula, roquette) is a leaf with a peppery flavour. Often used in salads.

Roma tomatoes (egg tomatoes, plum tomatoes) are favoured for canning and drying because they have few seeds and a dry flesh. Ideal in sauces and purées.

Saffron is the orange stigma of the crocus plant. A very pungent and aromatic spice. Use sparingly.

Sambal oelek (chilli paste) is a hot paste made from fresh red chillies, mashed and mixed with salt and vinegar or tamarind. You can substitute it with an equal quantity of fresh red chillies.

Self-raising flour (self-rising flour) is plain flour with baking powder added.

Sesame oil is available as a light yellow oil with a medium flavour or a dark brown oil with a strong flavour. Use sparingly as the flavour is very strong.

Shiitake mushrooms are Asian mushrooms with a dark brown top. Available fresh or dried from supermarkets or Asian food stores.

Sichuan peppercorns are a Chinese spice made from the red berries of the prickly ash tree. The flavour is woody and they have a strong, hot, numbing aftertaste. Available at Asian food stores.

Snow peas (mangetout) are a variety of garden pea, eaten whole after being topped and tailed.

Spring onion (scallion, shallot). These immature onions have a mild, delicate flavour, and both the green tops and the white bulbs can be eaten raw or cooked.

Star anise is a star-shaped Chinese fruit made up of eight segments. They are sun-dried until hard and brown. The flavour is like aniseed.

Thick cream (double cream, heavy cream) has a minimum fat content of 48% and some brands have gelatine added to them to give more body.

Tofu (bean curd) is an excellent source of protein. It comes in varying consistencies, each suitable for cooking methods (follow the recipe). Fresh tofu doesn't have much taste but absorbs other flavours.

Tomato paste (tomato purée, double concentrate)

Vanilla essence (vanilla extract) is made by steeping vanilla beans in alcohol and water. Look for products marked natural vanilla or pure vanilla extract and avoid the cheaper synthetic vanilla flavouring which is made from the chemical artificial vanillan.

Water chestnuts are small, rounded, crisp vegetables, usually sold canned.

Zucchini (courgette)

d

e

f

recipe developers:

Alison Adams, Renee Aiken, Roslyn Anderson, Ruth Armstrong, Rekha Arnott, Julie Ballard, Vanessa Broadfoot, Janene Brooks, Jenie Butler, Jane Charlton, Rebecca Clancy, Judy Clarke, Amanda Cooper, Ross Dobson, Michelle Earl, Jenny Fanshaw, Justin Finlay, Sue Forster-Wright, Kathleen Gandy, Jo Glynn, Sonia Grieg, Jane Griffiths, Lulu Grimes, Fiona Hammond, Vicky Harris, David Herbert, Katy Holder, Malini Jayaganesh, Caroline Jones, Eva Katz, Kathy Knudsen, Jane Lawson, Michelle Lawton, Michaela Le Compte, Pamela Le May, Valli Little, Barbara Lowery, Nadine McCristal, Dianna McLean, Tracey Meharg, Kerrie Mullins, Kate Murdoch, Christine Osmond, Maria Papadopoulos, Sally Parker, Kim Passenger, Anna Phillips, Justine Poole, Wendy Quisumbing, Sarah Randell, Kerrie Ray, Jo Richardson, Tracy Rutherford, Claudio Sherbini, Fiona Skinner, John Skinner, Melita Smilovic, Margot Smithyman, Dimitra Stais, Chris Stefan, Barbara Sweeney, Michelle Thrift, Angela Tregonning, Jennifer Tolhurst, Alison Turner, Jody Vassallo, Maria Villegas, Lovoni Welch.

home economists:

Alison Adams, Laura Ammons, Rekha Arnott, Julie Ballard, Anna Beaumont, Rebecca Clancy, Ross Dobson, Michelle Earl, Justin Finlay, Jo Glynn, David Herbert, Justine Johnston, Michelle Lawton, Michaela Le Compte, Valli Little, Ben Masters, Tracey Meharg, Beth Mitchell, Evelyn Morris, Kerrie Mullins, Kate Murdoch, Briget Palmer, Melissa Papas, Kim Passenger, Anna Phillips, Justine Poole, Wendy Quisumbing, Kerrie Ray, Chris Sheppard, Fiona Skinner, Tim Smith, Margot Smithyman, Michelle Thrift, Angela Tregonning, Maria Villegas.

photographers:

Jon Bader, Craig Cranko, Cris Cordeiro, Roberto Jean Francois, Joe Filshie, Scott Hawkins, Ian Hofstetter, Tony Lyons, Andre Martin, Luis Martin, Rob Reichenfeld, Brett Stevens, Mil Truscott.

food stylists:

Janice Baker, Marie-Hélène Clauzon, Jane Collins, Sarah de Nardi, Georgina Dolling, Mary Harris, Cherise Koch, Michelle Noerianto, Sally Parker.

food preparation:

Alison Adams, Amanda Biffin, Rebecca Clancy, Jo Glynn, Justine Johnston, Michelle Lawton, Valli Little, Ben Masters, Kerrie Mullins, Kate Murdoch, Briget Palmer, Justine Poole, Christine Sheppard, Angela Tregonning, Alison Turner, Abigail Ulgiati.

The publisher wishes to thank the following for their assistance in the photography for this book:

AEG Kitchen Appliances
Bertolli Olive Oil
Breville Holdings Pty Ltd
Chief Australia
Kitchen Aid
Liebherr Refrigeration and Wine Cellars
Sheldon & Hammond

Published by Murdoch Books®

Murdoch Books® Australia
GPO Box 1203, Sydney NSW 1045, Australia
Phone: (612) 4352 7000 Fax: (612) 4352 7026

Murdoch Books® UK
Ferry House, 51–57 Lacy Road London SW15 1PR
Phone: (020) 8355 1480 Fax: (020) 8220 1499

Managing Editor: Rachel Carter
Editor: Zoë Harpham
Concept Design: Michelle Cutler
Food Director: Jane Lawson
Food Editor: Christine Osmond
Photographer (cover, chapter openers and special features): Brett Stevens
Stylist (cover, chapter openers and special features): Carolyn Fienberg
Home economist (cover, chapter openers and special features): Jo Glynn
Nutritionists: Thérèse Abbey, Dr Susanna Holt
Indexer: Russell Brooks
Picture Librarian: Genevieve Huard

Chief Executive: Mark Smith
Production Manager: Kylie Kirkwood
Publisher: Kay Scarlett

National Library of Australia
Cataloguing-in-Publication Data
Simple Dinners. Includes index.
ISBN 1 90399 222 2 (cased edition)
ISBN 1 74045 134 1 (pbk)
1. Cookery. 2. Quick and easy cookery. 3. Dinners and dining. 641.5

PRINTED IN SINGAPORE
Printed by Tien Wah Press
Printed 2002.

IMPORTANT: Those who might be at risk from the effects of salmonella food poisoning (the elderly, pregnant women, young children and those suffering from immune deficiency diseases) should consult their GP with any concerns about eating raw eggs.

Back cover: Prawn laksa, page 131 (top left), Peanut and lime-crusted tofu with chilli jam, page 176, (centre left), Chicken, mushroom and almond pilau, page 208 (bottom left).